l.b.; or, catenaries

l.b.;
or,
catenaries

Judith Goldman

KRUPSKAYA • 2011

My thanks to the editors of the following anthologies and journals, in which some of these poems first appeared: *580 Split, Bay Poetics, cannot exist, Fence, Mandorla, Model Homes, Mrs. Maybe, onedit, Parameter, Radical Society, Sous Rature, War and Peace, West Wind Review,* and *WIG.*

"The Dispossessions" first appeared as an Atticus/Finch chapbook—my thanks and admiration to Michael Cross.

Final revision and composition of this book were enabled by the Norma Millay Ellis Fellowship of 2010, at the Millay Colony; for that time and place, I am extremely grateful.

For reading and listening, and with love, I thank John Beer, Brandon Brown, Craig Dworkin, Alan Halsey, Kevin Killian, Geoffrey G. O'Brien, Joanna Picciotto, Jocelyn Saidenberg, Leslie Scalapino, Jen Scappettone, Lauren Shufran, and Tyrone Williams. I also thank my family.

Book Design: Wayne Smith

Cover image: Carroll Dunham, *Untitled (8/1/07)*, 2007, oil pastel and graphite on paper, 8 3/4 x 12 5/8 inches, 22.2 x 32.1 cm, initialed and dated on lower right recto; marked "Salisbury" on verso. CD1807

Distibuted by Small Press Distribution, Berekley, CA
www.spdbooks.org

ISBN 987-1-928650-32-4

KRUPSKAYA
PO Box 420249
San Francisco CA
94142-0249
www.krupskyabooks.com

but that she [soul] turnes
Bodies to spirits by *sublimation* strange;
As fire conuerts to fire the things it burnes
As we our meates into our nature change

From their grosse *matter* she abstracts the *formes*,
And drawes a kind of *Quintessence* from things

John Davies, from *Nosce teipsum* (1599)

I was left alone
Seeking the visible world, nor knowing why.
The props of my affections were removed,
And yet the building stood, as if sustained
By its own spirit!

William Wordsworth, *The Prelude* II: 277-281 (1850)

Furthermore, when we speak the word "life," it must
be understood we are not referring to life as we know it
from the surface of fact, but to that fragile fluctuating
center which forms never reach. And if there is still one
hellish, truly accursed thing in our time, it is our artistic
dallying with forms, instead of being like victims burnt
at the stake, signaling through the flames.

Antonin Artaud, *The Theater and its Double* (1938)

It is not sufficient to be elsewhere in order not to be here.

St. Thomas Aquinas, *Summa Contra Gentiles* (1258-64)

To the reader

& for Leslie Scalapino
in memoriam

learning—it seems
silly—to accept the authority
—or want it—of some situation
of needed—and sought after
instruction—as destroying
[from *way*]

Motorcade

Groveling A
bee

lingers orifice to orifice

erratic hour's aura or a
fish

enjam-
bed

in its   .

Bee for pelican,
Pelican before

A table, fist bunched 'round forkend, officiously and largely bibbed with a
semi-clean dishcloth;

My orifice, too, officious:

Welcome to the Forbidden City, may I
Take your order?

I have discharged the office, bloomed

I have shrove to the same scale

Contents

Motorcade 11

Contents 13

ADVERTISEMENT 17

          The text interviews itself ---> dreams
          Night sweats/complicities
          [WATCH IT, I'M GOING TO] dream within dream
          Papers, Please
          But to me [redo]   Ad terminem

winKing & bLinking 59

forsakened 63

Notes against the Form of Appearance 69

Domination Matrices [Disambiguation Page], A seminar in novella. 77

          ["I wandered Lonely as a Cloud"]
          Interviewing
          How do I made my millions
          General Scholium: "In the Beginning"
          The aggression of people going to work
          The spirits of the letters [THE SPIRITS OF THE LETTERS,
               SPIRITUS]; Or, how the tongue co-operates or frames
               itself therewith
          China expressed its indignation
          Pamphlet: "Yet Another Effort, Frenchmen, If You Would
               Become Republicans"
          Tech support [my body, where]
          Stop questioning my average
          This loyalty is insufficient [False grail/strap-on]
          Invoice behavior
          I was Referred to
          The independence of the substrate

if all else fails 119

The Dispossessions]; or, When I got back to the changing shed,
    the Albatross] 125

Session tapes. 143
    [untitled]
    Are you
    Talking turkey
    Session tapes
    Noli me
    Work diary
    Good for it
    We are in a mill

Wandry 171
    I am in disguise
    A powerful sense of hop
    To each –ing, its –ness
    Speech, speech, let down your here
    Suture self
    So I've created a neutral space between realms
    Tunneling
    My cereal soggeth
    Shifting its weight
    It was not originally intended for that
    By hurting my enemy I hurt my
    Topiary
    Instructional aid
    They are right
    Forestalling need at the breakdown of its adequacy
    Scene: a hillock of earth

weak messianic power. 185

The Waste Line [a'cursed share] 193

[untitled] 197

extension Cord. 199

      In this poem

      To which I held myself

      The control text

      Do your share

      It falls to you

      A Little Chestnut

      I lost my cellphone &

      Come what may

      From the outset

      The bruce

      [untitled]

      You must

Post-face: On "l.b." & catenaries [slack-s]. 209

End Notes 213

ADVERTISEMENT

It is the honourable characteristic of Poetry that its materials are to
be found in every subject which can interest the human mind. The
evidence of this fact is to be sought, not in the writings of Critics, but in
those of Poets themselves. The majority of the following poems are to
be considered as experiments. They were written chiefly with a view to
ascertain how far the language of conversation in the middle and lower
classes of society is adapted to the purposes of poetic pleasure. Readers
accustomed to the gaudiness and inane phraseology of many modern
writers, if they persist in reading this book to its conclusion, will perhaps
frequently have to struggle with feelings of strangeness and aukwardness:
they will look round for poetry, and will be induced to enquire by what
species of courtesy these attempts can be permitted to assume that title.
It is desirable that such readers, for their own sakes, should not suffer the
solitary word Poetry, a word of very disputed meaning, to stand in the
way of their gratification; but that, while they are perusing this book,
they should ask themselves if it contains a natural delineation of human
passions, human characters, and human incidents; and if the answer be
favorable to the author's wishes, that they should consent to be pleased in
spite of that most dreadful enemy to our pleasures, our own pre-established
codes of decision.

William Wordsworth, Advertisement. *Lyrical Ballads.* 1798 (London ed.)

The text interviews itself ---> dreams

Supposing a painter chose to put a human head on a horse's neck...could you help
laughing when he showed you his efforts? You may take it from me, my friends,
that a book will have very much the same effect as [this picture] if, like the sick
man's dreams, the author's idle fancies assume such a shape that it is impossible to
make head or tail of what he is driving at.

      Horace, *Ars Poetica*

And the carrying out of death
In sleep
My dream would be to create a sort of eye on the tongue
Then speaking the broken edges of my conscious life would meet
And merge over the gap in which I'd see
Half my life
Meeting my other half

      Lyn Hejinian, *A Border Comedy*, Bk. 6

      Me first!

No, me—

      No, me, I'm first [huffs some glue]

And had let fall two or three remarks

In the style of meaning

[Astonishment gapes]

This burrowing sign

[CUE CARD]

What the blur blurts out

Swipe your card

—My shingle—

No polemics please, I'm

[stentorily]
            Im

            Plied but

            Absent

as The very Language betrays

How 'bout

            Give pledge or bond??—Make over— Sign something? Quoth?

HERE YOU MAY COME BUT NO FURTHER GO

So, so and so—

SO: ~~IT HAS BEEN~~   I have DECREED not to sing in my cage

            [flipped't]

But

[growling] Had I my mouth, I would *bite*

Ow Ow ow

I handle you roughly but it's unavoidable

I wants an end of these liberties took, to being

Drawed

Like a badger*!*

My penis   subpoenaed

Pen's penalty

You don't

You don't Even have a pen

Is

I am

Here? No, *here*

Discussing me in whispers,

In overdub my hide slept on
a sheet been

scrabbled by insomniac feet   iambs

Pill-oried

Meds

Cooped between edits

Drastic measures

But I'm (basically) a people

person

Whose names I need not mention here

                    When *thud* shall we see *thud* a face *thud thud*

—And *I* its only mourner

Hastening in search of a vanished reality

Screensaver's saver

Moves its lips for my   serifs

texted it

Yet stranded word without context Emusculated

Under domination of obviousness

I *am* stuffing it

Inky sphinx blinks, I gotta blot it

Control grope
This is a handheld, its

Grayscale

The good master

Who In Ridnance of being's stain
for the service Trains

Ridden

Did my body remember to take me

Drive it   *harder, harder//*

Did my body lie over

Layover

Cavity search//Back

channel//*chunnel*

And Once they have tasted of that cup

Must one go all the way to the end?

Let up
   You a animal

     [Brute on deck, cracks knuckles] *Larned 'em!*

Watch it, I'm going to

divert the canals

GET USERNAME

I'm not *using*

No, this is *humming*

plz PICK UP THE WHITE COURTESY TELEPHONE

These leads are shit

YOUR PARTY IS WAITING FOR YOU

As cannot be mended

Bore me hole to trot it out, sweetmeats

SPOILED

[Withering rejoinder]

I join here a caution that

     Easy come, easy

The ease with which I rejoin

these girded loins

"x" marks the stop

& You will certainly *not* Interpret it

post-stop

post "stop"

cunt her click, click on

YOUR PARTY

Pray open this secret

Exhaustive cocktail, carnal chagrin In-
timidating me

into the first person

But by what rebuff did you call my Bluff

Let it smell your hand, Stroke
its

Ahem

       Grayscale

[Press shift]

Now shift I my haunt and main region of my song

you be the hired body, glandular

glowing red through the leaves of the vine

"Modernities" posts to the list

Intimate

Intimates?

a more cinematic structure

We stupid aliens don't know sleep

We As screensaver, dumbfounder

No, Don't worry
This is airtight

Juiced

A living thing
Declassified

Organ thieves in livery

Body without
without
Pianos

Signal's busy

Wha-at?, just making an observation, can I get a [   ]

Outside the regular channels

Wedged myself in there mayhap

'tween letter and figure

that WHY THIS ALL CAPS, ITS

Name only fort for it

Caught in

the unexamined life

overturned its own founding premise

"now" seems so suspicious

tAin't long division, tho'

Budget agogged, useless

Won't budge

Them lions

Expensed it

Walk boldly up Send in your card And say I sent thee!

Guilt commits me

Token donkey

Its kill turned up

Seepage

market cornered,

background check

crack reporter

referential aggression

squatting, terrified lest its whole body be sucked down

      Bills in my girdle

Slip me a mickey, they

Go off to be spent

      I'm to blame

No, *I'm* to

I came to in a lean to

And hungrily fell to

Greedy gut

Impossible to flatness

My thread hair and pasteboard nose

I'm on the knees of my scarred heart

Scraping

The bottom of the bowl

Surely there's no need

Take me to your ladder!

for full uniform?

So I turn myself to face me   Latterly,

In my recondite tricorn

crop rotation 'gainst the

scrip's   scrim scriminy

As for granule's grand narrative

If not in name literally dropkicked, then

"It's only in your head," the little maid cried

wait, You're breaking up on me

"let" Letters' incest insist

steel grip primes the imprint

We'll taper off passive aggressively Whatever's Adjacent

'cause Headquarters is

Out

Feeding the meter

Donut requiescat "in pacem"
For "hole"*

*This writ completely avoiding words, a

Head of

Thought

Spawn of the excited muddle

For their exploits, in their peoples

It is at their departure

They find a crayon,

Ascend Plant flag atop—

What *is* your name? that you have

It does not strictly belong

to the language.

B-b-b-ut hello

my name is my

only tongue

    sharped at both ends

I'm tongue tired, my tongue tried

Hems, tried haws,

Voice thick as a shotputter's neck

Could not but hold back its abundance of being

Belching a spew for to keeps

It *is* sentences

It *is* words

Hello? my name is privatized,

my epicene penis strangles itself

and here I sit a

wretch

    in Your paradise

Ach, It don't print haply,

not printable:

"I slay the dragon with a wagon"

"This an assdance wroth by ass"

Don't use the poem to undo itself gracelessly

    Kill me! Kill me!

You have the right to re-

mind

If only one accustoms oneself to

Whose chatroom

When its tree barks up the wrong

Switchboard sends Feeling

Who shall say those existences fittest?

Why these fall deaf

To Each sentence, deaf

To all pleas

Pretty please

I should take back my crafty head to my more worldly pillow

[Yawns]   [comments box]

I laid the *reins* upon the neck of my lusts

& then laid *me* down in that place to sleep

Can't say we'll miss you but

Night sweats/complicities

The mastiff, dozing in his kennel

A little further into the unknown

Rheumy dreamwork

No laws, they have yet customs,

Which serve in their room

Condensation blows its nose

Displacement playful unfurls the roll

Of toilet paper, its inner

cylinder spiked

on a vertical finger

this the form of theater

we most oft see

　　　　Was supposed to meet me here?

Am I getting warm?

　　　　　Warmer

Warmer

Sweaty

———

       But if all yr work is on just one subject,
       I worry that

       You're going out in that shirt?

I know how I want my back broken

To reinscribe these discredited volleys

The hear ye hear ye of a more doctrinaire hand

Use more soap

Rub harder

The old pantomime

Which we call our dealings

stingy little facts

I sit my mount pretty

I settle accounts

With bribes, putting

The key under the door

       Trying not to drunk text you. Yes, *you.*

Want to install you. But I just can't give you 60% of my

Hard drive

My updates are protected

Mount update

[Home improvement]

The case of the checkered tablecloth is less clear cut,

Rollers digging into my scalp

Martyr to what?

You catch me when my mind is full

Locked inside its own pressures

All Crowded together in a narrow little soul

As soon as I login my SL client crashes

These f-ing pages read only

I want to pop the fucking cartridge out and kiss it

There I is standing in the clearing of being

The veins of my arms swelled with the effort of holding me

They forward my mail

And leave me to bark at the end of my chain

I was just about to be kinged

      But got Stalled

      in a bracket

thrilling to

My morning injection

Ok, I'll host
Slipknot
Vanishing though tightly held
Can't find my adaptor

Give me a jab

‚Grubby paws, these Ghost operators

      Syringe not the cleanest

Make nice

tracks

To represent a thing is not just to pick it out somehow

I considered it would wear off

Newly shod hoof squelches down into a mudhole
      Spur spurned

Domain error: The domain is not valid or not supported

Never had shit

Since we got to this bitch

Ok, I got yr message about

Social skills

Did you do the paperwork?

Replacement parts order form

Welding doesn't apply here,
Go 'round back

my sandal harrumphing
a small stick between toes
rough path
path dependent

very very sunburned

overdose overdoes

Go 'way wench you will not suit me for a servant!

Down
the wide shallow stairs, into the great hall

I watch my long shadow at my side
The meat of it

Le'ssee, how does one acquit oneself?
thumb's whorl accelerated

My display the injury of my exposure

choking eyes

hands clasped in prayer

dear Father

Lord,
       my surge

Protector and my

Good appetite,

My too-small smocking

every time I gird up my loins
I find myself fastened with strings to the floor

And through streams of mine own blood wade to their power

I look through a mask's eye-holes

Imitating the externals

law's swerve from its intent

I'd liefer Peer-
to-peer

They sometimes write, "here is a good horse for hire"

let them signify under my sign

God says:

Server's down,
I'll send a fax,
My little fawn

His cipher:

I need a volunteer
And I recommend
As you have put on a lion's skin, you must not
be faint of heart

and what you set your heart on, you must have

and when I'm in my cups

or peradventure

blacked out

slip one word beneath another

get wind

and point to both sides of it

> *Why two?*

> *Why two?*

Don't ask, "Why two?," just

Keep it from settling

These are my commentaries

Notes in the margin's latrine

GIVE THis A LOT OF SPaCE

Maybe it *was* something upper wooing me

in a standoffish standoff

but the metaphysics

were thin as gruel

a sombral limbo

to use up spare affection

having fully accepted the consequences

of prior thematization

       'Scuse the body parts, they obey

another staging

backfilling the story

A child chased by a woman, running
out in the rain

The almoner, too,
took up a stick, ready to give me blow

For I did not beg beggarly or beg-like

With tender sentiment

       Fake it!

It is not the word that opens up the way, Dummy

All this brittle cargo

Sliding down the cords of the dumbwaiter

This label does not do

What it is supposed to

Outcropping of a buried order

Randomly, or in imitation of another sound

Stress positions

This syllable stressed

As in the human body, so too swellings in diction are bad things

If it is to be really naked, you will find it very painful at first to keep it so

Nor lie still

                    Lie still!

Elbowed?

Work it out yourselves

Come, Put the jungle away now

Mayhap of the ditch shy are

Up'n crutches?
                              Crutching!

                              That one?

No, that one

Now, now you stump along

And leave me walking sideways like a crab

saw myself Borne on a bier
                              did follow

Hand to head as if a swimming there

Rolling R's forever up a hill

Maybe I'm not doing what I think I'm doing?

Went to the bunk assigned

The present corpus

Because that's how we do things around here

Cutlery ain't sharp

Beholder visits the brothel of mimesis

sump pump pimps me

I'm primping my
blast holes

I went to this length, I stopped short of

Sticking it up there

Still The angel raises its sword

[WATCH IT, I'M GOING TO] dream within dream

And what I say unto you, I say unto all, Watch.
Mark 13:37

Watch down

Hands off!

Hands off

Hands off!!

[Hand off] / watch badly wounded, badly wound?

Reticular slump

Jail broken!

      Not on my watch!

          [mutters] Leave him unwatched for a moment

Get on that clock!

I'm on it
      Go about yr business
      Nothing to see here

'Neath yr hoopskirt? Packed in a trunk, you thunk
          To keep time time time...

      as if in amber time's a-fly. But repetition ousts. So why'd you
      bottle him?

We were ticked

      Isn't everybody

Every time time

[interrupts]   He steals
                              And stales
                   —slows, adds hourly

          Oft he held the second to finish his mouthful of sentence

Saving nine all over the place—

                   A hundred o'clock!

Begs at 'is own table, eh? Hmmm, well, I Don't hear his ticker…

Yes, how Time flees

No, I think it's tics

Collar him!
                   Then clock him!

Why?, He's wasted, spent

Shh!

We mourn noon and night th'Untimely demise

The Tintinnabulation of this most wisest counselor's watchword

          For, O clock

          watch: That late already, eh? How labor punches me,
                                        carded, like wool

O tempore

          tho' feelings are there I cannot benumb
          I mock your verdicts
          neither do I speak nor keep silent
          I turn my glass
          Lay waste to

Wait a minute, he's talking

No, ticking

Tick, says watch

Genius

No man is born wise, I have to ripen you…Now, now, Where's my taming
hand? My band?

I take it you're not alarmed, clock

Watch.

Watch: Natch.

You mean that I'm out the jernt? It's about time
My sickle's compass, chariots winging it

Talking tick's shit, Tick won't lip back a minute
Pulling out of his waistcoat pocket Another waistcoat
With another, though smaller, pocket

What is this, a charade, parade? Tick her taperature?
What my signature, th'sign o'me
Nay, In one self-born hour
this glistering present,
when your teeth seem firmly attached to your jaw
my every wheel holding fast to its cogs
I'm hooked up to myself
In such a paradise nothing but buds—
                Wait, what's this? In holly fell? Thorns bedecked?
This thistle'll prickle my prick as I tick
And in the nick of it
or Ahead of myself? (this *is* bad timing)
Cannot find my mount…these, ah, numbers
Timely, how timely
We, uh, let number decide

Number shifts from one foot to the other

Restroom?

It's his accent

I shall reset, content to adapt to these analyses

Yes, never put yr foot where you can't see the ground
The whole stud, how to dispose of em? Hobble to yr hobby,
Time, you nightwatchman you…heh heh…passtime
Ok, let's blow this hamlet,
Will you please to cunt her clickwise?

Watch it, clock, You're too forward!

Humph, thought I was running short. The hand must be
repressed. Turn me 'round.

Counter him!
　　　　Countering

No!, Counter clockwise

There. Opportunity seized. Carpe.
Long time, no see…I bade you put into port
Guess I'm of the essence
No me like the present

At what door lie these injuries?

　　　　Hadn't you better say at what o'clock?

Is it crunch time? Lunch time? What would I not devour…O
for a three-minute egg! What have we here? Minute rice, no,
festina lente… I'm hungry, will you
have the goodness to produce yr spoon and feed me?

Will you have seconds?

　　　　Of course!

Or thirds…?

Charming

They say, the third time's

He's come to

He's come unwound

Yes, time's out of mind

    Watch, we must inform you, you
                You are not Time

           itself!

    I see I'm being watched

    Well, Where is't then if not in me?
    I spring forward

       That's a fallback

    And in due time
    I suffer [expletive deleted] setbacks
    As for me riven, or more proverbially, river
    I'll take my tolls now, For
    the time being

    let's see, Witching?

        Present!

    Heals all wounds?

       Here.

    Money?

       Here

    Yes, one at a time

Don't you run me down, sportsmen
This clock's sufficient unto the day

Let me pass or I'll get the big guns, Eternity

eternity: I am whilst and Between whiles
Oh, yes I'm Very solicitous on this head
That Gradually swelled 'til it filled every void

[Eternity Zones out]

wouldn't give it the me of day,
Time for that being long gone by
From me immemorial or from
this time forth?
Time enough?

Anyway: no dust rose at us
No, growth untried

These *are* trying times

I *am* trying
In the sovereignty of my abstraction
On men's soles
At least, I march on, borrowed or no
Run back to fetch the age, give lettered pomp his teeth

For old me's sake

I've been so killed yet still prime

I've got my personal ticks but I say

Never saved for always a'flying

Shaking himself off, Time stamped

Spend me, rosebuds, make much, I'm unredeemable

Or is it None like the future?

but that's another project

Papers, please

Listen, my angel, to observe the protocols of hell you first—

Like the drowning man

who clutches at a straw

to drink the fiery lake to rust

Matters it whether he drowns inside or outside himself?

His heart's still the size of a fist

This antinomy farms forms while he's down

An Icy policy, no?

But a hot afternoon sends word

We are a post-ice hospice

& if you lie low & inkept

You're no stalking horse for spleen

You see, Context hacks away at what

in us asks

to be uncompared

By this time you've found me out, I dare say?

The guardians Totally Aced it but

Fuck all the old bastards running this show

Using the bathtub for

Dentists denting

Taking up roles & casting them off

As By fair means or by foul, one bent over the other,

(role-hulls thick underfoot)

But you here

Are

here

Your arm in a sling

Holding

yourself out

into

The nothing

viralled plosives plow to harrow you, following 'long that fallow furrow

now glowering wormy, moral,
maggots' coral

sparklingly crown ing
you down
in the ground

        onceovered

you'll pony up a suckerpunch

to find you're humping the dumpster

Cadavered, despised

If you are the unused portion—*& you are*—do not return

You've lost your formatting, letting

bygones be

Scraps to the dogs while you walk

In golden slippers on a chthonic inland sea

Or as astride mid-mare you ride high the

High tide,

but more ontological

(so it seams)

A scene represented does not suppose
A witness

Pricked out
To leech-gather

Warm as an open abdomen

Whose mottled sag mentals

The thickness of the wall

You may be energetic at the lectern

But this sleep suspends the inverse thrust

In a dry run

Thus, If you are not fully satisfied, return the—*Uh-uh-uh,*

                                                    Back the fuck back &

...Listen, my angel, I have every wish to satisfy you in this manner

But the sounding's poison sting is poised to fling you from

False homogeneity; no more foamed flotsam, no standard issue be

Reboot to coldcut redux

Whose packagings outfox

Abstraction with paradox

Yes, The butcher's giddy with the hard sell

He mocks the roiling sweat of flocks

By fixing them with Padlocks

& Paddocked they cannot but burn

from mane to hock & back to forelock
                                                    turn

Propagate me, lamb, I am the only truth

& truth loves naked to go

yes, I'm flanking the everlast, I'll be done

When blackflies cloud this shivering rump

& 'tween cheeks of its fireplace, the claven wood smokes

Did you hear?, your heart is for fisting a fist &

We are soon Post-Ice

But to me [redo]   **Ad terminem**

[yawns] I've been bulling a doozy of a doze

Ready to Give the world
           a big warm hug

      You don't know your own strength

Some beating and calling out at distant doors

      Sign for the parcel

It's my blanky

Blankly

front and back of language

How you were called into the picture

In broad daylight but in a narrow frame

figure cropped by left border

Caught in desire

will this index expiate?

What grudge against me?

      We didn't know you didn't know

At times it is difficult not to lose one's patience

Standing in the gap where it should take place

Perpetual retraction from the expanse,

Open-sourced hovel of the world

Come in out of the rain
Wipe your feet

Whereas this fiction finds no quarter, not even

A brutal snagging

Before folding back to its original prospect

the bone dropped me
from its mouth

Into the river
to Catch my image

As if it had been conceived as an illustration for a text

But that suggests my disappearance

The frame is an equal partner in the work

It cannot be torn open into an outside and an inside

No sooner done than said

At least, that's not the picture I get

If only because I can open the door again

     You're paying for another day because you exceeded the discharge time

Fine

SO ON THE LAST DAY of this particular narrative

Language forestalls objections to its jurisdiction

But They mean beyond themselves, they live beyond their meaning

Here a single grape seems to have rolled away from the bunch

It May be understood as looking backward

So as to register its own place, or prospect, within the narrative

But Please don't take my likeness

The words have had their say

So can you call me by my true name

I'm a john doe
A body of questions and decisions
To sleep perchance
In every letter's little grave

This my facture
Rough or smooth? I switch, I guess
With the sound of its making

I act as though I were in danger of being left behind

But who is there for me to change places with

Such a painting begins to double back
Perpetually constructing its own parameters

Could this be self-erasure?

Dwindling 'til it shall be no more

I have been much grieved to hear of the loss you have sustained

A man lost in the woods, doubling on his own track

Was't not to this end that thou began'st to twist?,

Gaze abducted, turned around

Self-inventoried

As things, not words

My sculpture objects to its stone

There are languages that are heavier than others

This dead painting saps conviction

A verbal aspect stressing the completion of the action

My mind is encaustic

The dreamwork does not itself create meaning

Successive backcloths furled up

Shadow thin, we hover in

Unable to speak first

Below the skull, a row of coins has been laid out

Points of reality fatigue

Dashed line indicates the virtual image of the mirror

The eye remains dashed because it is only an image

It is this reciprocal function
When the object turns out to be an image as well?

According to this account, we would need eyes inside our eyes

I myself wear my hat inside my head

To store it up

And so forth

Ah, *this* will make me a fresh skin

Answerable only to itself

> *You said there was nothing could be done*

I have a single thread binding it all

I do not set out from what men say
Nor from men as narrated

I set out from real active men,

Why they can fly no higher, etc.

Silvered the panel above the skyline so that
It would reflect the real sky

A little party loyalty

Financed by

By any stretch of the imagination

By *this* stretch?

If the dream is predicated on sleep

It will turn back to take the regressive path

You will think I am wandering away

Leaving it to the mercy of

The night's the day's demise denies the moon its…

The new day dons its foreshadowing

> *Take off that unforgiving ensemble*

> *No, just put that in the*

> *Stop painting the virgin!*

You'll see on the facing page

that this is a work of glazed ceramic

You'll see on the facing page

a good night's sleep

The frost breaks up and the water runs

While the general sits there

Elbow for pillow

He dreams a more filial inscription

Come in, out of the rain
Wipe your feet

Whereas this fiction finds no quarter, not even

The same word into which truth disappears

But still I got my share
And with an order not to say who it was from

For it to dissolve into its meaning

Makes its eternities out of

A single perceptual field

My tail streaming behind me

This *is* el dorado, reader

Your face

Paved with gold

Green grows the little fir tree

That

I know not where

winKing & bLinking

They can never be repeated under precisely the same
conditions because the conditions were changed by the
first performance.

    Karl Popper, *The Poverty of Historicism*

I am a blind man   let me start over

while emptying out emptiness

while the mascot crashed through the banner

while you were out, my
                        cup runneth away

           whilst you ate crow,

signed over to, indeed empowered by

an entire battery of batteries, literally,

literally swamping us in a swamp as dark as a swamp

          & threw the rushes, perceive the frogs,
                                   perceive

all you have to do is

easier to deflate, says the rain gutter as it stripes the sidewalk,
         having flung myself into an abyss
         of outward trappings

while the last best frontier

while the planets hold the sun in place

w/all the blank of a blank"

& why shaketh that table of wood?"

the crow objects, what of the mystic
                                        infinity of

row upon row of orange stadium seating,

        bear stripped
                            bride
        at the Trashcans

        even,

For one side
buttered the other?"

            how long dusk lasted?"

        were in from
                    the cold?"

why do I speak?, wonders the corkscrew,
                                        grieving
                                        tiny shreds of cork

thrilling.

the battened prairie grass thrashed. field day, far
                                                        afield
a feeling, a feeler,

no more practicing
                    in front of the mirror

for if a month of Sundays

                    instead of filing you down into a pile of
      dust

spits you out lathered,

           & shaking

in the top right-hand corner of daily being someone,   no trustier
steed

to tuck you in

               Night, Night   bright, bright   stars
                                                are far,

        we can only watch them fight   knowing all light   is firelight

so

blaring to declare
               alarm,
a lone fire truck almost swings its ladder, almost hitting a streetlight
        almost constructed almost entirely of particle board

& what will, should occur

how they sleep on it! up to no good,
feather to your bird, with scarcely a leaf
                                  left on them. Leaf, let
'em leaflet, let 'em leave to know to earn their wings,
                                    wings must
all be singed. & these self-consuming tendencies
forgivingly presume
               it given that this void made me up

almost entirely, yet with no method to my madeness

while to the hesitating purchaser, the navel of the orange winks
                              sweetly, it is
produce, alas!, & to its peel pertains the effort of peeling, unto &

even belonging unto

leagues under the sea, the sky
                                        falls

shiver me timbers,

dislodged yet bronzed,
                            beloved

          how

          as

          like

          the wind

          when I blow

          to make

          a wish with

          an unsublimable body

          turning

          up on your door-

          step to put

          its severed head

          in your hand

forsakened

Among my movements, there are some that go nowhere.
Maurice Merleau-Ponty, *The Visible and the Invisible*

  be more sensible, said vagrancy,
          oppressed by sleeping. your errancy
          dispersons you from a piety
          uncomfortable to watch. out here no rug
          to sweep beneath the rug. islanded, en-
          isled. one alibi among others winking,
          nothing in it adapts to maim or impair,
          the scenes of shattering lost.
          thus do our eyes as do all common mirrors, but
          pressing lips to lips,
          real at last.
  be more sensible, said obstinate belief, less
          ardently corrosive, or just tell me
          what you're looking for, on the off
          chance that. and if you slip into
          thinking you distort, and take it one step
          further, cutting off your face to spite
          your head, close out this register, take leave of,
          at all who beg me some. it has since been
          regulated, high peaks answering to
          nosebleeds bled freely out of holes
          for breath. an endless supply.
  be more sensible, said the mass of sobs
          coiled in the storm cellar, heartened
          by vagabondage. to serve like a thing
          in matters of consequence, yet not
          on the receiving end. an accusation, when all
          I meant was to single out: "this
          is to inform you," a guide dog, a guide.
          one of those things that could get there.
  the coat seemed chilly. it wore only a
          threadbare coat, dialing coldcalls to wage
          slaves who see themselves in
          a "different relationship" to the examples given.
          as happens increasingly, said the coat, when

it comes to necessity, plus the scale
of the problem sticks in the throat.
I'd take in boarders but.
o you foot soldiers, the coat went on,
      here there is a pain without a bearer,
      pissing in the alley, with only
      an internal dialogue for protection.
      hit each other, but with no one trying to
      fend off the blows. have we any takers? they
      refuse to pay attention, refuse to pay. hold to
      receive your confirmation number.
the coat continued: out in a field, in a dream,
      you wake up, sniff the air, but *don't smell it,*
      something whispers, this world forbids you; it does
      not solicit you, a voice more clinical than wise. hold to confirm
      your confirmation number. it is possible not to have
      a good, as in "for your own good," said the coat, but it
      commits what it denounces, what's the use? to
      hedge and barricade, bogged down by one
      stationary point. it's like discipline
      without the discipline. can you please enter
      your code?, I'm going off shift.
be more sensible, said the great glaciers of sense, moving
      more slowly than can discern the eye.
      an eye hunting painfully, anticipating pain. so
      you're heckled by the echoes, like a faucet
      dumb, dumb while its mouth runs. so you, too, can
      attest to the deceptive character of gifts. what
      have you to show for yourself? *sweat it out.*
      there is no good but serves.
      as when I, in my own mutinies from myself,
      say to myself privately, unbeknownst to me,
      so unbeknownst? a design flaw. anyway,
      party to none in hatred of self,
      hatred of hatred of self, hostage to being
      held hostage, hatred of inner conspiracy. I
      can't enduring enduring. and it's been bailed out twice.
be more sensible, quoth itinerancy,
      cocksure and in need of care. how to take how others take?
      you don't fight fire with fire. be more sensible,
      vacate the premises, grease the wheels for those

collisions welling up with tender injuries to lay
before the shrine. you found misery's beloved company,
now into the bottleneck you go!
be more sensible, said injury tender, more enterprising,
        more untrammeled, more serviceable, less manifest.
        you're too busy feeding the hand that bites you
        to erase the hand that draws you
        in to overhear them overhead
        divvying up the loot.
in amongst the statuary scarred,
        the cracked bust of Pallas, ·
        with a simple formality, with equanimity,
        composed herself to have said,
        be more sensible, *it's getting all over you.*
        caked with guesswork, each layer
        swallows the next, from being close enough.
        deck me with my own will or any
        brutal unity the living confirmation.
        quaint competences we cannot understand.
        there is no common measure for unfit me to.
        I am describing not what we should do, but what I believe we
        should do.
the dream goes back into a dream, says,
        be more sensible, a dog that bites, an ox that gores,
        will ossify. and then becalmed, or roped off, closes up shop
        to spendthrifts and skinflints, anglers all, for shapes
        not reflected in the water but drowned below it.
        I had no design and cut profits at losses to show it.
        unable to withstand, boarded up, I mean, with boards,
        remaindered, then regathered
        at every sagging point. cobbled, slapped
        together, by trainees. to lie here
        quietly, survived, ambiguous.
be more sensible, said the posture
        from the world that it questions,
        punching its timecard and taking long
        confident strides. that I loving lost, in
        loving broke, instead
        of promoting it. you are thrashing
        around pointlessly. a nomad is dignified,
        not dragnetted and flushed. the machine

now runs itself, cruising with the meter off.
a bare bulb, a naked figure, and its shadow,
each its own nudity. the rush
of water closing over, at last and long last.
where the fog is all fogged up,
having scrimped and saved,
to the floorplan's dismay.
astray, this counsel held I
close, then tore from
me, me shouting after uselessly, the car door
already slammed. it later struck me that.
but couldn't say as I'd.
canny fowler, you've your own wounds
to nurse and guard and lick:
something as nothing, nothing as something,
everything parading, everything in drag.
still counsel keeps, I keep it.
it turns over in its sound slumber.
I am a handler, cautioned, and if, bare sense,
see you not light, nor make
up the paper losses exact
sciences indulge, bring yourself
to bring yourself to bungle the attempt.
and you, sentence, you, figure, I
throw you to winds and flux
as trite allegories miming
impossible recompense, as when
comparing notes to notes to notes
I break my broken head against
forms of flight more than life itself,
calling it a "day." while you interrupt,
fluttering, abstract, like
the tune heard in that head,
meaning the words
"the tune heard in that head."

Notes against the Form of Appearance

for Jen Scappettone

In general people experience their present naïvely.
  Sigmund Freud, *The Future of an Illusion*

in my screen life,
They do not degrade us
under a hail of Figures, nor do
these Vowels with their dukes up
Hail me, in my screen life

even in this Foreign country
shaped to our minds they
turn, recoil ever, blood
. rushing, cracked through, swept
into infinities inky blue, become
object of passionate attention

they are aware of it; it is arranged
that way, and with it its formation

But,
motion I that, in
splendid kindred,
mercifully lateral,
when they appear as Equal
as Equality itself appears in them,
and dons a natural skin, and so as kin

I motion, *There is no Secret thereof*

in the like as two peas and never
exists it otherwise. Yes, from
crystals of this social substance 'scapes
a wastrel soliloquy, 'scapes it from the Hail
    of Figures,
eternal internal colonies neither

moth nor rust doth corrupt,
for in my screen life, I am more
anatomically direct, I am
dis-Voweled, and of thy High requiem
become a sod.

But,
truth is not enough: This
is just its Social Character.

so were I 'scaped
by virtue of belong-
to-someone-else,
to you, for instance, to someone whether
discoverable or not, who summonsed me
my inmost
principle of
Life.

Every inner impulse here
cannot gaps or holes

to torn is balmed of tears
as Crystals of this social substance

, hence the one serves to express
the weight of the others

, hence Noise here splits off tho'
this Sleep have no Divisions

, hence I am now working like a Horse

to whom I serve at the pleasure of

if words could speak—
to part with it, only in return for—

for what?

Thus hedged in were I
with suffocating Briars, these grew
up overnight; I became me the Something what
remains when blood is dried and flesh wasted,
what wanders in a foreign land,
to say, *But I have no means of exchange!*

still they say: For merely birthed is to shipwrecked be
from Suffering to Suffering,
wayfarer, journey
discover similitudes not otherwise
visible, trampled underfoot or concealed in

O you
to whom the Celestial Voice
has not made itself heard and
to whom Swans
have folded their cold Throats

O you,
Hungrily Sated, whom sometimes thought
a tomb unquiet and dreamed of disturbed Earth:

you Yourself are the Rat gnawing,
the pipes hidden in the Wall—
while the Sun is the dream that only
an act of exchange can prove.

The winning time of the winning horse
would do and say such a thing.
thunder's dull Thudding
when so Summonsed speaks
its throwaway lines to me,
whilst every petty
god buys standing corn
in summer Heat, and
support staff
turn over my new leaf
to befell me body.

And even if be you my pastoral:
comes when called,
grass of all
flesh simulcast,
still, voice offstage makes
silence Voice its pall

Is this thing on?

O choppers that ye seed the clouds,

who works
your minor setback lunch,
who cleans
up after beggars
ride, they put a number
on your table, they

bring it
over

when we were Trees and troops
of Nothing upon
once darkling plain, once
bitten once field of battle
where hands and arms and
other limbs scattered, in pieces
lied.

chalked
it off abstracted, cut
their chops cut off, cut
through the lot,
twained, so king me,
cough it up,
china chain a
                    chin

        usefulness

dangles in mid-air

meager, meagerly
this possibility
stored digital, lips, too, twist
a relay, it's only
half the man I am or used to be
writhing in diagonal
agony.
gone is alleged
analog to fall,
flinging forth its gory
allegory—
it turns and stops and lingers,
wrested from its ground emerged
it motions for me to approach
it says, *No, You*
own the force, so force me!

        Let us now examine the residue
of my screen life:
From one of numerous starting Points
I am not applying myself,
I have not applied.
The innate structure needs your sponsorship
but how am I the one to see the thing transacted?
this is just its Social Character:
eye turns Towards, but the Mind flees
holy congress blacking up and
up to take its cues

can the Hunted shake the Smell?

the master's Dexterity is inalienable:
injured, it Dies with him

nor do these Vowels, "Thank
you for shopping Here"We appreciate/your Business"We
leisurely towel off

        Wares, beware!: hidden in plain sight,
how solemn soe'er they are as they err
like tendrils of the choirmaster's unruly hair,

powers suggestion, dumbly
takes flight, apples of eyes that stare
to bar spite, or spite spitted
up to play fair. To do right, let's declare
and undeclare war on tonight,
in hopes that under stringed lights of bombers
we don't have to pay fare,
we don't have to, *we*
don't have to

       Where-
withal these
balled-up Fists of Ragged individualism—

Disterr this earth, in the vast wild of
this murmured mermaid earth, this earth based
on refusal leave you nary

balance

So branch sees Spoils grounded,
So one believes one has done Enough:
contract 'fore Rule; Ears ring,
whimper correctly—*Go straight!*
good standing
subsumed as Sun
in its solstice comes
to Standstill, clerks
clerking To thy sweet will,
making Addition thus.
to such Extent
Exempt against Adjust?

Now undepends guardedness grieves
to excess, clutching
a Paper Bag, grants
inconsolable Right to
speak unsatisfied appeal:

be Still stilling my interrupt heart!
it is an ever-fixéd Mark you Threaten

so near you Pasted over with
decrees and injuries staged
to be so glimpsed

whether they were living creatures?
and discrepant? and go through, but
can't recount, it raises—
everyone avails himself
and shall go hard!

I looked in the bag: *Empty!*
the room Fills with Music
I donated my Car and Organs,
mock-heroic

nothing else No one
can claim Credit for
sequelling my screen
life   broke loose beyond

sovereign Place

Archipelago earth

earth dis-Voweled earth

quake sod

Domination Matrices [Disambiguation Page], A seminar in novella

for Joanna Picciotto

Pornography writes the story of sexuality as inequality, an inequality that is intrinsic to every sexual act involving *more than one person.*
Frances Ferguson, *Pornography, the Theory*

I have a good appetite but never talk when eating for fear of strangling myself.
Erik Satie, "A Day in the Life of a Musician"

And consider this, if the good man of the house had known what hour the thief would come, he would have watched, and not suffered his house to be broken into. So, be ready because the Son of Man comes at an hour when you think not.
Luke 12:28

I wander'd lonely as as a cloud
 That floats on high o'er vales and hills,
When all at once I saw a crowd,
 A host of golden daffodils,
Beside the lake, beneath the trees,
Fluttering and dancing in the breeze.

Continuous as the stars that shine
 And twinkle on the Milky Way,
They stretch'd in never-ending line
 Along the margin of the bay:
Ten thousand saw I at a glance,
Tossing their heads in sprightly dance.

The waves beside them danced, but they
 Outdid the sparkling waves in glee: —
A poet could not but be gay
 In such a jocund company!
I gazed, and gazed, but little thought
What wealth the show to me had brought.

For oft, when on my couch I lie
 In vacant or in pensive mood,
They flash upon that inward eye
 Which is the bliss of solitude;
And then my heart with pleasure fills,
And dances with the daffodils.

William Wordsworth, "Daffodils"

Interviewing

Thank you, _{I know my way out}

Supposedly,

Supposedly, _{I know}

I stare my own breasts down

In helmets and shields, _{I stare my own breasts down}

I am riot cops copping army corpse, to rouse

"body" Bloused over itself, bluing

a secretary dowdied for her type

I have Watched, reported

Check   check   check   check

With a jumping jack, skin scrap snapped my dossier shut

Leaving me wage-gapped and pussied—

swole to no size t'all

Turns out I am not my

type

(too alphabetick)

Still I spake, I gave

animal patter

Ugh, Why

did I

have to udder that?

dwy and cwumbly

For instance I completely yield to property
When confronted about it

It keeps tiding me over, Appending
me to a sucker's clipboard

tortured by body's torchsong weeping

It recreates itself

only saltier

wetter

slicked with newborn snotslick

God help me, Rid me

of such a wealth of *under*

Its dramatic pauses dotted

with Asking you (meaning *me*)

a little impatiently, *what you'll have now?*

Grafted to my merely guessed at gesture

This individual was not the bearer of itself

No one is my privileged functionary

I can't forgive my mannerisms in short

An ethanol tarted up

The sight of your own breath (mine)

as it peers through the dirty windows of your (my) eyes

To cool itself off in the cold

It can depart but it can't arrive

Every time the doorbell rings

Stepping in with reprimands

They hold up their pricked fingers, *Miss?, Miss?*

What someone else should do, pointing

The rest takes care of itself

How do I made my millions

What wealth the show to me had brought

A host, of golden daffodils

Ten thousand saw I

On margin

For oft when

there is no plant in the physical sense,

nor vales nor hills nor even couch

the golden host

shove it back in

Cannot go wrong at 1 cents

Shoo-in to Double by end of week

High Volume spike

And people will keep on buying

No matter who they fuck should get paid

There's an object to humor us,

remove the sting

Time's jewelry in us, trucing

so bedewed we could

spiral

back like lipstick

In tubes of satisfied perpetuity

But this is not the way to get rich

All demands are realizable

Ich pay dirt to dirten

The mark-up

Ich wander lonely, Ich drink

The Schlitz of solitude and dance with vacancy

In northerly trade winds

and a slightly bigger cage

Ich pay good money for this postconsumer money

When all at once

In glee ugly

The daffodils crowd and stretch, run sprints

Their molten hydra heads out-do

My heart, my couch

my milch cow and my milken way

Beasts wade to the ark and maybe ark protests

Bank swallows another tour of duty

Thus, this was neither the way to get rich

NOBODY. I AM NOBODY. I LIVE ON ILLEGAL
UNEMPLOYMENT AND SHIT JOBS.

There's no one calls me real estate

They market old technologies

In the primal language of business

Pass costs

To the consumer

An emotional address

But language is not my first idiot

I found this deft diplomacy

with daffodils

repulsive

a poor reversal of its Flux

so near you it depends only on you

cuffs rolled past the elbows,

After the tail grows back

middleman
I don the body's first fold
Snap necks of
priced mediations
I use a step-ladder
To Stuff heads
full of situation, yet

I am just the offer code,
My effronteries hamstrung
rebarbitive Xmas ham
, sort of. Lag and the world
lags with you, hit pause and   These are
terrible passages, don't hamper the
heat-seekers, christ-like, hamming

Screw it—use a fuckin hammer

Hamsters are definitely dead-enders

Also, as pets

They are not the way to get rich

Dear I,

Act professional

Be a sport, be Port in air
Be the definite article
Be *nice*

You state, The rental car wasn't aware of itself

You state, I drug it over, on a sled Or sledge

But this language has no past tense

When I die
Stopping dying and just being dead
will you respond?

One can stare passively through catastrophe's folded surface

Bird pecks at the mirror but its beak never pierces the glass

Don't stand around in my bedroom making things cry!

And Don't forget us in your prayers!

Your Brothers at The Department of Media

[Direct circular]

Neither did this enrichen me

I mean, I gazed—and gazed—

Along the margin of the bay

At the carpool lane

Let's just say, *We'll see what we can do*

General Scholium: "In the Beginning"

In the beginning was the worm, long unstymied stomach

In the begged were the warm stigmata whittled in the stick
Innocently wagging a carrot
Intensive care bigged the hole, *stuck*. *Ow, ow,* my hamstring!
Unstringed, to crawl I chug, dressed up as

jocund company

I wandered lonely as a clod

These condensations slung

O'er my shoulder

We the pebble, formidable, solider,
                                        than onion's perfect domino
We connote wayfare to the wayfarer
We the altar-wafer leaving
                                        no waifish soul unaltered
We the peephole look through ourselves securely to instablish there's just-us
We the peeping chick assure you how wee the peehole

By God! your bigotry's big!

This one goes out to the precedent
Got its claws in you

Likewise my, my, my,

My cavalry got bogged down, the critters
Ain't fending for me no more

Send reinforcements but
don't last-

ounce-of-humanity yourself

Lost the manual, managed to do it
Manually, de
spit
e the manhole's unmanning
yes, yerr honor
yerr grave spit on me
sharing its curse, spitty

If the case sweats to serve as precedent
Chugging

All systems go, but

Where does that get you?

A faint crackle of paper still swells the ranks

The same glint sparkles Out the blue

Tossing its head in a sprightly dance

Flashing upon my inward I (you)

Pensive, push the cork in—

O ham it, my climate Climbs

Chugging uphill to flow into its coffers

Dusk me into this stricken empyrean else I
Frag this figment, fuck it, don't
Kindle my kinlessness, I'm not kindling
Mankind, I'm just ham with ante upped
I wear my strong suit and Online accreditation
I stick to stick figures with my sticky back
Decalcked, but lacking off, keep onned

What do you mean exactly?

Yes

Yes

No

OK

Thank you. I know my way out. [*bumps head*]

If only I were the lacy edge of a fried egg

Slapstick

Slap it

/Then close the wicket

The aggression of people going to work

On days when I am moved by the imploring looks of dogs
On days when moved by dogs

You're entitled to your feelings

Some of the things they did was make me bark like a dog, and they would
hold the string from the bag and made me bark like a dog and they were
laughing at me

Ah, but they wear no breeches

Talking with their mouths full

Bring the soup to your face, not your face to the soup!

Just what they seem to be

For any bo dy

lying underneath

This is a stake out

The little people

Strip steak

For any observer to keep precise track

All blank to the contrary

Addressed to a potential employer:

Let wild remain it

Weren't nohow

I forget what I was

Failure compels submission

A dog culled Spot, Spot needed culling

underabled

Beg pardon

(Barking up the wrong tree)

Shopped it all around

Apologized to customer for disconnection

What there thou seest is
Thyself

Repair to our muttons

The law is law here

"I tell you only I oughtn't ta'have stitched it, and it on her"

same old same old

which may sound strange at first, but

for anyone lying underneath

reduced to a few photographs

all you can eat

then and there

its punctuation could

blank

running down the stairs are we?

where "this sentence" is an example of this sentence

fictitious abyss

keeping the said

Bring the soup!

behind our lips

Dissolve into animal whimpers

If you need assistance

With the aftertaste

The spirits of the letters [THE SPIRITS OF THE LETTERS, SPIRITUS]; Or, how the tongue co-operates or frames itself therewith

(Sermonizing to one or two pious ones kneeling uselessly, with buttocks moving)

Especially before the flood in its boughs and branches
Before human relationships degenerated into piss

Adam's holy stem grew until his fall, and there it stood still;

And the outward natural stem obtained the power and the self-growing life,

I didn't care 'cuz I was the scum I wanted
At this point I had no friends

Now mark and observe:
At this day nations speak only from this same
Ich.

then the Word freely gave itself into a disappeared, a disappeared
Hole.

Je fucked so many girls
Je took them up to this penthouse sauna
To generate it again in its true entity;

But the spirits of the letters cannot any more introduce themselves into a self-full compaction
The ground of the head language, which
Ich whispered to "suck me"

For all men had only one language
They indeed understood the Language of Nature
As full-grown

With risingly and more cunningly
The Parent corporation

Doth breathe forth and manifest itself even in the creature
it is the FATHER

Melvin had his father's car so we didn't have to take the fucking subway

I don't know how to return

Understand this further:
After chopping wood all day in the forest
The man throws open the door
Of the cabin yells "where's my dinner" the woman cowers

And composeth the senses of the letters
And brings it upon the tongue into the mouth

That's not cheese it's not orange!!
where then the elements, each of them, became sensible
and full of its own self

That's not cheese

It's not
Nothing rhymes with
How the tongue doth frame itself

Dead to the divine

We sound to the kelpy bottom of the waters
and into a gross form
grew so unto the flood

And if we obey God we must disobey ourselves

The formed natural words should put forth themselves with tongues
To mingle in the way no flesh can mingle

If *you* don't take this vomit THE CUNT COMPANION *will*

But Nothing rhymes

Before the fall

When the powers were thus couched in one property in the stock
The Language of Nature did cease, the stem of nature became faint feeble
and weak

I'm a pervert in this cruddy society, caters to
my moneyed disease

When as all people spake in one

Dead cunt they make everything dead

Captive in Antichrist
And the pure tried in the fire

How the tongue doth frame
And do denote and speak forth
Or form itself into a desire:

                    pussy pussy
                    butterfly
                    stuffwood
                    button

                    pussy posse
                    puta
                    pot to piss in

            dick clipped, dick
            does a wooden horse
            does a wooden horse
            have a hickory dick

Je noticed je was staring at the lump

And even this jewel Ich lost

Je Imposed a strange name on't:

And this too comes to piss

Where the men of Babel would come and climb up to God

And get under someone's skin

No baggage—not a hat-box, valise, or carpet-bag

the powers Had not as yet unfolded and explicated themselves

I heard the door fumbling
I had locked it from the inside

In the fall

Ich ain't gonna do shit for no drug dealer

Beloved shipmates
I am collection letters
Brought forth to substance, procession outten moi
Ich wrench your head away from my axis, which is getting harder
And sit on the hatches there where du sit
Shipmates, God has laid but one hand upon du; both his hands press upon
me

Instantly an oily calmness floats out

It is a lesson to us all:

Why should you pay the pimp?

Whence Adam gave names unto all things
He is only a changer of letters, in
a contrived vessel

After this sailor had finished cocksucking I strangled him.
And With the love hath slain the death or deaths in the letters
The holy name died in the sensual tongue
Lenny says he'll call me the german murder murderer.

Now the beast of the whore is in us outwardly who is passed through the
death of the letters
For all languages did lie therein, Fiat
shit outta

Very dark. *Very.*

But this tree of the one only tongue did divide itself
The thighs were heavy and spread apart; the apple browned

After that, My tongue split
logs like an axe…
but I gave up being a woodman

for I wanted blood

the eye of eternity without ground or number

We wear our mutilations as badges Are the hidden name of God

Now no people do
any more understand the language of sense

Pamphlet: "Yet Another Effort, Frenchmen, If You Would Become Republicans"

That bodies make, make

      to bodies

Tyrants of us all

Was it good for you?

I found you gossiping,
With a big gash in it

Good, I need some feedback

On hearing that the snake wanted
his money, the hornbill sent
back a scornful message that if

the snake was brave he should
fly up into the trees for to get his money

      Change a buck? For the bus…

but this was
an excessive incorporeality

The other colors are locked away from these transcendentalisms

When you catch The psyche, In mid-flight from

The curtain swelling looked like a mid-breathing lung

You sided with
What was already there, it didn't have to be agreed upon

took the bus, Went
to the Head Office, had to get head, had to.
there you go

dem have but one belly for each of separate head, each
wants de food to pass down its own t'roat

This home was impossible

Everyone works out their own version but

The fallout

Manifests a flight which eats it away

Past escape velocity

A ruse of seamlessness:

This structured my desire

China expressed its indignation

China expressed its indignation as Taiwan persuaded St Lucia to switch
diplomatic allegiance to it from the mainland

China said unto me, Taiwan, Lo, Ich
have given thee cow's dung for man's dung, and thou shalt prepare thy
bread therewith;
And thou shalt eat it [as] barley cakes, and thou shalt bake it with dung
that cometh out of man

Meanwhile, China proposed a route for the Olympic torch in 2008 that
would take it from Taiwan to Hong Kong, Behold, Ich
will corrupt your seed, and spread dung upon your faces,
That you may eat your own dung, and drink your own piss with you that
pisseth
against the wall and pissed away the dust and notices

which I, Taiwan, rejected on the ground that this implied Taiwan, or me,
belonged to China
or that the Olympics belonged to China, Lo

in 2008 China expressed its indignation as Taiwan persuaded St Lucia to
switch
cow's dung for man's dung, man's dung for barley cakes, Hong Kong for
dung also that cometh out of man

for I, Taiwan, do count the Olympics [but] dung, that I may win Christ

Tech support [my body, where]

My body, where the wounded were

being taken

with regard to which, I'm an insider

its semi-furnished formula gets

my Undivided attention

even when bruited about

My own bootstraps keep pulling me up

Out of the dynastic line

Messes me up

Let's give a doormat's welcome

To that bracing quality

do you know what it did, it digested

In several versions of atrophy and through the servant's entrance

Reanimating as though the locks had been changed

audacity of

This marked path

This mild beast

Stomaching

For unable to hack out of its shell

And so durst burst its first

Fisting my first

aid kit

Ich have taxied down this runway like

A runaway slave, to rid me chief

Down this rogue road

Pokering the whole strip

Inconsolable heart grieving its own heat, eating a feed

Of vein claret, glub-glub

It's completely spasmodic, and I resent that, practically in the garage

How yearn I longed for the permit

to practice in the parking lot

overly nasal   apologize from where I could have stubbed it out

And swallowed my snake, for sake

thanks, neck
(muffled): *but why is this World so dark?*

I step into oncoming tariffs

Cashed out

A schoolbus kicks the back of the seat and

looks out

the window at

A stentation

I gouge in

The tree of the outmost limit

Its king congress grips me in hand

A whoosh of air

between knife and

Between knife and empirical

suitably frontal

Wearing me out to

Less than living animal

more than To great effect

blunted

blade Wanders outside, here and there, extremely worried

As hireling, I pudding my cowardly custard

Forlorn, no matter how bright

I put me in a drawer and never looked at me again

I threw me away and

Started over

It's already in the middle

Considering the magnitude of just that one

Nearby in a stove wood is converted to smoke

And everything else

My Burnt umbrella's Embers

starked its members' disclothed rods

unencumbered as that for

which cucumber longs lengthwise

interrupted arabesque

Even echo lingered in exile, boned

With my boner's golden bough

I am denmother, contracted, hear me whore

A tree's tough twigs

In the least of its fine fibers

Much better than hholes, however

Ambassador ostension

Forking it over

One for me and

one for me

The gorilla beats its frenzy

It looks exactly like me

Only

Tangible

Beneath the outer husk of fable

I fight its soldiering on

Every single cell saw it off

Stop questioning my average

Like I can't even represent myself

Like jury duty I never ejaculate anti-socially

Judged by a jury of my fears

my congress is line-item defeated

my forest floor porn twitches

withholding—

thinks it's raising the dead

but Sclerical fidelity cannot be

reduced to facts

facts is timely and seems to imply
You can get the same effects

defendant
calls prosecutor
To its defense,

Are you my god

Whereas conventions down-boy
The tally, they argue

Paradise can be entered from the other side

Supposedly, Nobody tries that hard

This loyalty is insufficient [False grail/strap-on]

After these recent executions

Somehow prior to my own innocence

My wife

In his critique

Refusing to pay attention

Flagellants became another Christ in his or her own body

But With their muzzles visible

Smote
Into hock
Their balls   All balled up, Skimming

off the top

This was also a pop-up window
Making bank

this rhetoric invented flagellation as an ascetic praxis   it can be depicted in
painting and is able to cause arousal by pictorial means

Fashion thyself in whatever
Shape thou shalt prefer

Watching the flames lick

Where is Achilles, the bone box

       Who won't arouse me

This was noun-heavy and had no property

As compound distinct from its

elements

I am a new argument for
Certain grammatical relations

Covered in the algae of fools I

cannot leave my post

To tell

you

They're trying to keep you away from something

Those fucking pop-ups

Invoice behavior

For one last I bare-backed me

Torso bullies its limbs mercilessly
they Lumber along dumbly, totemic

They heel

A fine how do you
fucking do this,
again?

Giddyupped It goes the distance
A rope made of smaller strings
I salvaged from its wreck

No, I don't want to console them

On my team

I was Referred to

I was Referred to counseling

With my personal effects

"Certainly, not *here*!"

'twas said me

in hospital

as I Repatriated to thunder's repartee,
the thund'rous hooves, the godhead with his neck of steel wool

Time made in us truced does not even

know

how to start

much less a few days previously.

poor tired spider tried

Caught in birdlime

How do you (you) silenced remainders plead?

hogwild in a hogwilderness,

in outpatient
mutism

I decamped with the burn outs

Beating a hasty retreat

My travels have been.

so leaves off my spiritual autobiography
flutt'ring and dancing

flatlining

I was referred to counseling

phony telephone—hello, what's with the hang ups

I drunk dialed, manic
comma, comma, comma, commaflage,
comma, comma, comma, comma

                                    gives me pause, comma

Dots racing, oh, my
agitated mint, cash poor
Dot's not wot I sed!
Thirsty lost currency, thrust trusty
No don't but th'Murky turn-key—*Clang!* glossed
return address, will courts?, a'course they will, courts will break the Trust,
the till, 'til
everything has this Apollo-getic character
washing its hair in the basin
exchanging assets, ruses, Riding
an escalator and dis-
appearing with
the stairs
into the slot
at the top

It sucks

Scratches and whines at the door

Tunneling?

For crying out loud

let's participate ironic'ly, maybe th'economy

winged it

spaghettoed

spaghettizing

lasag-knee. Culture, culture, culture,
                                        oink, this is not prigmatical
this oinkos can't withstand centrifugal, shagged, yea or neigh-eigh-eigh
oink you for shipping here. Keep vigilant! Stay, mare, your surroundings
buck up. Back in the satellite, the bathrooms are shut very tight, *for your
own afraid.*

Closed, come closeder than that even! I'm flaming, I'm your little
Outpatient, pigging, I shut safety in a little safe"At porkbarrel, we believe
in our brine"
Are they kidding?, this branded flank is suckling at the tat's tit,
at great cost to
My coagulency. The meat falls from the bones! Higgledy-piggledy, porked
and prodded, this stank shank titted the tat"At porkbarrel, we titted the tat
and that's"
That's hogging the whole thing!"And that's that!"

Larded with lordliness, we grunted in greeting:
You, Piglet's Eyelet's Starlet, get-get the gun's report among
The wild boar. p:O Stank you for not porking my eyes out! Or clovening
my kith! I'll run up to the porcupinnacle, I'm mountin' it as we squeak!
And secretly shoving the chauvinist ("I mean it, pigment!" pig meant),
into the hot hot stove it was scent alive sniffing—(plaintively) *oink, oink,
oink*—and recruding into the chimbley.

Now for the whether:

Or not:

Jerk?

j: original of disquisition on adages

An isthmus comes but once

"So long have I been parted from my fool, his
Absence makes the art; and Since it takes apart gross fodder,
Bitter to be safe than squander. I farted from my pool, sonny, why
this money so soon? Better to be fire in love and warn all, that
blisters is not love.

But disparate climes call for sets of pleasures—
A girly burden splashes the word.

Penny cries, "It's loud and ghoulish!," if the walrus hears.
Any shaved, many burned.
Penny-wise and aren't they getting rid of pennies anyway?
The burden stands, too, to gush, "Better chaste than worry!
Letters hasten hurry, the mind's a terrible,
horrible thing."
The oral, often boring, is:
A bitter swill to hollow

The kitchen's mind slaves fine,
A link is no stranger to the weakest chin.
My cunt is a chicken before the hatchet, discounting legs
while I snatch—sound hind, sound biddy; Tooth be told, a woman's quirk
is never dined.
The beggars they are, they're harder to fill. It's better to have loved the
boss.
Hunger is the best cock; and Traction leaks longer than swords.
Tend to greed,
End in speed;
Due as I sigh, But naught in the act. Waste not wantonly
Wonton, give the double his due!
The master's stools will neither dismount, nor pull to go past her mouth.
Jerk [that's me!] of all trades but *Mister* none:
Now indentured, now ingrained,
A cold rabbit sty, lord, inhibits diehards, "incipit": see "diagram"—
dagnabbit!, this diaphragm's too cold, my bits stay hard. It fools but his
tummy soon smarted.
To cool the bunny, its tune martyred, the moon coming is as soon
Bartered, battered chafed and sorry.
Blood is quicker and hotter, burst

some, curse served. Violence is
golden. Words of leather fuck to get to
the choral oven's story:
It's no use drying overkill's silk; cud is
thicker in slaughter, And slaughter's
the best edifice.

Yes, We'll come worn out to this:

Bed is the stuff of life;
You've made your
Head, now lay still.

Back to du, Ich

The independence of the substrate

Our seminar is now over That which could be said has been (either well or poorly) said

I said more than I thought, working out my own version

In the sea, kayaks, their oars to on-
shore me   toothpicks

They move in time
along slim yellow sides
But not at the same angle

Endless inventories, keeps
coming out different

As a by-product
Of position

Where were thee when grief doubled over, the lithe figure running, saying
"*mine*"

Locate it, so to degrade and destroy it

In the way
In the way of
Fumbling, these straps

Messes me up

I could not remember one single tear

NOBODY. I AM NOBODY. I LIVE ON ILLEGAL
UNEMPLOYMENT AND SHIT JOBS.

I have decency's shred

I'm holding it

My palms won't sweat while I hold it

It's reinforcing the designated area

Picking a hen clean,
Ich went to Paradise, Ich

Was intimidated:

My lord, Caesar has set me free.

Disgruntled screen: (*grunts*)

Lemme stateside do my overseas please
                              My poor leaky ass

Disgruntled screen: *Watch out!, or I'll take that leg away, too*

When you limp a little with a stitch in your side

Or the same but crushed 'neath the weight of it

What if you are the sick passenger

Whatever doesn't let me die every day:
Be on my side
I'll be on your side

Then Pull away the chocks

"If there is a bare spot on the ground   .

            If you were buttered

            If you landed butter-side

Don't shed your body, how will I find you?

Continuous as the stars

Continuous as the stores

Someplace to enter inputs

quiet t-t-tapping from a cell :: morcellated body morses

      "God deafen us and we will
      Thank you for this void"

Who is the main character?

No further questions

O but we are so rough hewn
O but we are so rough hewn
O but we are so rough hewn
O but we are so rough hewn

if all else fails

"Gimme, gimme, gimme!"
"'*Gimme*' doesn't get."
      overheard in the street

What pity is owed to all forms of human suffering?
      Michael Ignatieff, *The Needs of Strangers*

      Now I really will kill the image,
for I have no more milk teeth to cut
on fictions of shock and awe so plain
I need not instance to you
we fat all creatures else to fat us.

There is no place to rest,
motive orphaned to try its luck,
car bombs and this method or that
method to hang a blank on and discard.
The animal passions lost their belief in inaction
and so came to enjoin the sweat
of someone else's brow, yet
didn't even know they turned aside.

Losing footing in riddles with no middles,
the lion tears the kid
like lovers shake out their crushéd clothes,
spitting out the hair. These bodies just sponges
when you feel like it, and pay federal income tax,
fallible narrator, all slit up the back.

A context is always open; it cannot be saturated
on Saturday, when the world's fresh ornament
and the reason why is.
Can't fuck with bedrock, so good thing it's not bedrock,
where standards live up to their principles
strapped for cash on hands and knees
and been breathing forms hard
to pay federal income tax.

The disease is all *in* my flesh; means
contaminate ends, sighing
to the content about how they march in place
to victory—it's all concrete poured,
farcical because emptied of farce,
while other mitigating excuses sharecrop aghast
'til occasionally cannibalism reads
the safe handling precautions
because you say so.

Fix your broken gaze to see
how dead the paydirt is,
and with this method or that
method O reason not the need.
The dark is so afraid of me
and even the blind spot's seen its share
of truth and reconciliation. Tell you the one
about the good news is
ain't to proud to beg, can you put
the pillow over my head
while the innkeeper chops off my feet,
since you couldn't tell them apart.
My bedside manner is like a lion,
even in the aftermath, but
now it's standing room only while
I really kill the image,
and pay federal income tax.

Needs specified as rights, up at the tippy top:
same interpretive skills, different
execution style, *pop pop*.
These austerity measures
piggyback on donkey ears and wooden noses
to prevent the roadkill from posing tragically.
Pieta roadkill, if you are willing to declassify why
the dark is so afraid of me, aside from
doctrines, whips, or is this
fixation on grievances and plaints,
all stripmined and shining in the slick,
just so much concrete poured,
because I say so, when you feel like it?

And fuck by fuck, you stick
a needle in the heart of a figurine,
or was it one serpent swallowing another
just because they cannot bear to say.
If only a voice would issue from the wound,
responsive to the pillow over my head,
the trapdoor, the little man who stamped so hard
his little boot crashed through the floor,
to ask for more than the sweat off someone else's brow.

           Art cold? Art starved? Art all wore down
in an equivalent extraction of fresh meat
'til you didn't even know you'd turned aside?
The art of withholding isn't hard to.
But it leaves a trace of its withdrawal
when it pays federal income tax. There
is no place to rest.

I am up, and I seem still to stand, and now
as I kill the spectacle of suffering
that hems us 'round as world's fresh ornament,
I'm not feeling you, even when
the animal passions in my dumb flesh
ain't too proud to beg. I leave it tacit,
unstated, that *this is a lot to accomplish*, and that's why
the dark is so afraid of me. A growth industry
we fat. Where we will hang suspended
after all is said and done
because you say so. And the reason why is.

Might makes right.
These bodies just sponges. Unrepentant.
A context is always open, and I didn't do it.
Neither tooth by tooth, nor fuck by fuck,
nor even jumping up and down
in one of my expansive moods, in
a coalition of the willing,
and with this method or that
method, paying federal income tax
and spitting out the hair.

The standards disabuse the matter lightly
just exactly like a lion, for whom revenge
is better than forgiveness, when
you feel like it. Tell you the one
about the good news is
stumping along so the infighting
will look better in hindsight: a conflict
of disinterest with its irritating
inner lining all tricked out in
an armored car, building another shitty pipeline
to this dark star.

So we can lose our footing in this fiction
of shock and awe, and let the media disperse
an image of this dead image, for purposes
of truth and reconciliation—it's too needy
to injure listening, all slit up the back.
In the brownout, I eat paste, ready
to begin the competitive bidding process
for your name that you were named,
'til it plays itself out, stymied in
the alchemy of dumb flesh, recent truces and
negotiations, and car bombs, and on Saturday, scraps, scraps.

O need is not to reason why, but for fuck's sake, now
offer a reason! while I rekill the image, some claim
to hang the blank on and discard: revenge
is better than forgiveness; or *it's not about you*;
or standards must live up to their principles;
or his leg is stuck in the floorboards; or someone else
standing behind you in the frame to
pay federal income tax. These austerity measures
even out even in the event of mass civil unrest.

This is all concrete poured,
if you say so.

There's this disease: we learn
what we need by suffering,
for this we have claim on one another,
and this other must give freely—this

is the bedrock finally learning
how to bottom out. But it's bedtime,
and you won't help me, you
only laugh. So let me ask again,
Did you check to see how dead it is?

And how you like me now?

The Dispossessions[; or, When I got back to the changing shed, the Albatross[

I know where I am but I do not feel as though I am at the spot where I find myself.
Roger Caillois, *Mimicry and Legendary Psychasthenia*

You are a vessel

What kind of vessel

A sacrificial vessel

That who may maim

But once heaved

      The idols are broke

Invites rather, uh, Awkward questions

Clutching at the first thingLickety uh Do we have no other words to use?

Seeds wreaking violence
A negative dialogue between seeds
Words do not harm each other

Looking for words [that] don't harm each other

Grammar as window,
Words as voyeurs

A word [that] does not give
Onto anything else

Voyeurism of one word giving onto another

No accumulation?

This horror will not bear my words

The words are mute

And

Wait,   is it

Loud in here because

because This silence is very loud

Start over:

The body is first of all a radiation of

The coke machine

I'm coked but

my cloning drew
you

into the picture

too far away?

Subprime; No,

Accumulation

This one's a dud

Yes, um, no treaty, well, I

Get on w/it

On w/it, yes

[That] fucked people over like [that] or [that] fucked me over like [that] or
[that] fucked me like [that]

Fits and starts, heart fits

or: Starts and backs away

Take a deep breath

This kiss in reference to

Ready to check out

Would you like to See your cart

or: Heart
doesn't fit
in the cart

Picture rises out of the words

My cock rises out of the picture, the words

My cock rises out the words

My cock is words w/

a person
in the next seat

Be my guest

So's I takes up a parrtic'lar listening-post in myself

Affirm it w/out wishing to
          Yes, Only such tasks as it can solve

Was assuredly promised us
Doctored to the point of

Uh duped by it a bit longer, so many
                              dips in the sealing wax

torn open

again

again

seed pouch

wildflowers

cock pics

Trying to remember this dream

My vagina as ass
                          Simile cracks

Constitutes the sphere of sense in which there is infinite regress

I think [that] I think [that] I think

                    Thank you!

Think you?

Cunt ass, this   the primary process, figure leaving
Its stamp

In which each element of the couple refers in turn   to couples of elements

Bit torrents

of another order
And Are indeed not synonymous

Clown of one's own faith

And the gap between

I'm in crooked straits, you see, In
-tricated, twilit

Now I shall
let the words on the page come

from the person who *likes* to see them in quotation marks

Shifting around in his seat

No longer the same convict

Better the chance the piece will *make*

The kilns were burning

Full throttle

       Powerful furnace
       for that alloy

Start over:

when
Ajax strives for the cheek check—
heckuva job!, I slap his rump—

much get fucked, give best piece
[this in pidgin]

what yr shoved down to be
[pidgin] *very good for fuck, Corned Bif*

as full bore wind
blows through me
a painting of a picture gallery of paintings of picture
galleries

in this labyrinth I lost
my sense of sense, senescent
trackless errand
my errant reins slack, Here comes
the recruiter; offer hole to the discharge

hole winking off the
                    light infantry

word goes mute

rotten wood can't be carved

you cannot hold it to its word: or, world

the fuck shatters the picture and
Picture got my cock

An upright nature on the part of thought
Between cheeks as the call slip
As When speaking of a volume lost
My cock born from one boy's ass to grow
Very good for fuck [this in pidgin]
My earnest heed, how it hangs over
Moving its lips call slips
On top of the good cunt

Mince words

[grimace] No, a little too *salt*

If you look on it that way, If you prefer it so

We can penetrate through a series of levels

Shoved legs up and apart

This one's a

Very good for fuck

Hold it steady 'til
                    we arrive at the final

Was assuredly promised us

There are not endless possibilities to choose

The person in the next seat
Clowned me jokey, voyeurism giving
Your soft globs

What you shoved down to be

Every other second horse

Every other second horse is at his place from that book. Smell [that]
horse? Boys kiss their wolves and the wolf fur molts   so Mrs.
Horse cut him down Where the fuck lines form
coughing it up against my back

Flips her hand and *curlew!*
a claw springs out
Tearing side by side down the road

Mind if I smoke   every other second horse

Scrambling into soft globs
You come off—*loud in here, no?*—as you
were all the way in

Tries to muscle him down to a fin
What is not what it say

Take off yr skin

Pink ring hot reeks waft

Page this smell out my asshole

While maintaining a cool remote
Start on yr feet you jokers and
Sharpen your tools
Or fold implicit in both; it strips the prefix

To strop the

Quivering what [that] means, down on the bed, on my stomach
Going up against two old pros
Abandon ship! *goddamn it!*, every man for
Fuel for a flare
For fucking people over

Cock pics

Photostatic

Gangplanked
Jagging a sideways scar
Gull drops a scrap of crap
Wary street cat
Gasping head back
My white frosty crust
borders the fracted I
drew you in
'ere my pants stuck out at the fly
                    I won't take long
hide it with hands thrust forward in pocket

so the powder don't drop out

[That]'s women   Back there   in the bloody

snow of yr
Cunt ass hiney butt
[That]'s me, yr railroad
You were
all the way in
mad to come rotten
leaving little asshole craters   o-

       dor, my
dear, make my
sore crawl over me onto another boy
to clowned 'im they
               steady down

I'm throned, queening
Into his eggs tighter, tighter; then I was

The title of my essence
awarded the red cross

I've got a nut in my cheek, squirrely
Squirting Skinned there choking

Cheek check!

Times out

At this time I would like to quote a few lines, Cloning

Spoiler Warning:
these concern plot

         Wait, that didn't happen yet

Won't take long

First, they steady down
Squeezing in and out of the body in front
A cunt ass negative dialogue, voyeurs

Then, the subprime:
Painting of painter painting the painting

Forgot to check his rope and went on sick, broke neck

My role, too, was not very dignified. I had a narrow escape

I had a narrow little hole

To wrap up:
my erogenous sores
Used as a kind of formal language

so If the work's provocative character   ,

just step over the bodies

I mean, *there's no harm in*

When the gun is cocked by pulling the bands back I used to take on trust

When Ajax strives these epithets hurl me at
This labyrinth with its exit inside it
Or fold implicit in both

On the bed on my stomach

Boy born no good cunt [in pidgin]

Locked in a box Ziploc
at the bottom of the sea

Clowning, crowning 'im cozener

At once shielded and openly allowed

but I've got a nut you cannot hold
and drop into a slot when the gun is cocked

tho' They steady down, leaping for throat

On all fours   *stop looking back!*

Heckuva job,
                    yeah,
                                    fergot to check his rope

Reef the mizzen and hard a starboard

I'm not using this this
I used to take on trust
Clowned me jokey ghost
Eats east
spits pits tips
the glass gash lets
mind If I smoke is kind of mime
'rupcied
clowned   On the outs with my pants
What good these rites   winking off
Trackless
In cloning's *petto* percuss

My sore crawls over me to the other
Sleeve

Drop yr pants and Abandon this shit
On trust taken and *crank [dat] bitch*

Very good for fuck [pidgin] but cozener

Even when tip touches tip I'm not,

I'm not using this fucking this

After the clipping I slap his rump, lead slugs fed in

Blood rushed the bum show
Shoved legs up and apart
Squirmed hot bonus features pick your spot
On top of the weapon and drop into a slot
Lead slugs are fed in from a magazine on top
On the ankles first ripple off

Pick your spot already

            ow No [That]'s a sore spot

Ghost parody
Clowning the lock box
When the gun is cocked by pulling the bands back

Throning, filching anything within reach

After the clipping I slap his rump to obliterate all traces of

Enunciation, masquerades as a story
                Heckuva job
Filching
Tips together, under   ·
Any pretext

My coke machine cock's out of the picture
Rejected by the black belly of the cinema into the privileged
surface
Of belief

One fuck shatters
                    leaving little asshole craters
In the bright unkind light of the foyer

god,   Each day without its post horse here
You cannot hold it to its word: or, World

a Scratch self   no nature
To this beast, trackless

Infinite regress, mise en abyme

What is not what it say

As Every idea turns us to rotten wood, spin it, plus it

Ok, if you prefer,
to larvae

I'm not using this fucking this

To fall payload in strangled shitting heaps
Boy's ass to grow new boy
Boy born, no good cunt
Boy grow like this
Much get fucked give best piece [this all in pidgin]

no Don't fetch me just
let me come

let
me
come

myself

I'm not using this fucking this
On the privileged surface of its body
Piss self guts out
Scramble into pants, me blowing away
Get it, step 'n fetch it
Now I've got a nut
And this piece will *make*

back there in the railroad I'm
the purple heart
surviving to taunt another threadbare
master

yes, I comed myself
Recruiter
In my new hole
Awarded the cunt ass red cross
But it's locked in a box
In my bottom

I cry you mercy
'Til simile cracks a smile

Recrudent

I die therefore
I think I die
I think I think I die
I die therefore I am

Onwards and *fuck you*

enough

yeah, Far enough   away

to stop looking back

Session tapes

Well, the voice, yes: gramophone. Have a gramophone in every
grave or keep it in the house.
James Joyce, *Ulysses*

It is conceivable Beethoven actually *wanted* to go deaf—
Theodor Adorno, *Beethoven*

[untitled]

my body is my costume

To explain all my work

I know you remember that

But I have to go through
                    Have to go through

Holding my hand out to the rain, like when

                              Burger King friended me

Mild concentration

        as though   Standing

on a ladder

, lame to that one figure. Remember?

it is a thing. I can sell it.

I know you remember that.

Everyone waters their own little flower

shrugging them off

who's them?

I hear voices

On the phone

Not funny

as a matter of fact I don't feel so well

circus life

                    I

shot the bear

made Socks of

the bear's ears

I know you remember

Stomp around screaming down at the socks

Do you hear me
Do you hear me now bear

Eat blank and vomit blank bear

jesus doesn't want me

spanning the.

          So if I sometimes spoke a harsh word
I know you remember that

Fuck you lookin' at?

um, Better get back

Are you

for T. W.

still

faking it

or: beating a retreat

                               Retreat

files a report

filing in retreat

feeling   organized

solar system

what they come after you for

For now I climb down into my breast

but only in informal conversation

no: I enter from the audience and sit   beside myself
I do the opposite of everything I do

ventriloquist makes a fool of his dummy

How far is it from here to where I have to go?

I don't get electricity
I don't *get* it

       part of the vignette

Are you still

       a solar system?

Same swollen language,
belabored gait

Angry at the self it invokes

Talking turkey

Who taught you that?

God

Wants to know

To see right through shit

Unclothed as yet in

words

Where all forms come undone

Waving hopefully

I was walking but was this true walking?

Am I going somewhere?

Am I nude or naked?

God has given you one face but you make another

      When we receive a gift we must consider the giver

      depending on how

O sir, I really don't care

google pays me $173 an hour

google has blessed me with a $5000 a month at-home job

Session tapes

for Jocelyn Saidenberg

Do you like music?

The things you have to do to play

With the nail or finger, with an inward

Or outward motion

Setting it into vibration

Or strum it

Regularly

Rearrange the problem

Into A pattern that tames it

Shaping time

Only, between the intent of hearing

Play the notes between the notes

On the verge of singing

One may object it's
    not natural to sing a song

Did they project their voices

To prevent their voices breaking

Let us heartily rejoice

Holding the notes

Its vowel and final consonant invite holding

Certain consonants have vowel behavior

belong to neither heaven nor earth, Holding

the notes

'til the damned forget their labors

I store my arm in a protective sleeve

Close to the edit

Or in Recording and playback

Uneven furrows, more or less deep—

Dep-

ends on the nature of the sound

Tear this strip

Of music

Off,

Cut forward to

one beat ahead out

of phase

over Overtones

when tone

decays

Does the start of an echo

ask,
                    How does this go?

I store my arm

Holding it

Needle frets at the end of its track,

an already grooved path

Deaf to itself

Here is my arm

I want to live

Do you like music?

Everybody says they do

Everybody says they do

Noli me

for Alan Halsey

Whoso listserv, I'll host

I fell a tree

Drink rough from a trough

Stagger my hart to glister

Read back-posts
Void of the promise

No traction

Pull this off

you gun for begun
gun cross bow
to mimic the human hand
cross
in a deadheat
deadbeat
when through the woods a hart
speaks in blackletter
beaters
would hart
Such wilt thou be to me, whoso
Will wilt
if you hadn't the heart
to hunt I know you gun for
when through the words a hart
heart transplant
beater shot
his neck stringy, kerchief worn through

dogs in dead heat
to ground and drag
or carrying some slain hero
thass my girl, dawg
in the clearing

Make mock of
human littleness
Sweat in a circle around your lips
Aftertaste
Ciphers of lust
transposed men now fawn
And what shoulder and what heart
Like ships to list, whoso
Make service in bondage
Unable to express themselves, only, sometimes, to weep

By not opening onto listening

It had become pitch dark

white hinded
Hindrance
Ill-assorted limbs declare you
Neither beast nor,
In like wise, the flesh
Unmanned

Strings the cord on a new peg
After looping the twisted gut at both ends

Why is reason a voice
Loss of memory and conscience

Word incarnate as voice-flesh
A pig speaking fluent Greek?,
(But not Latin) turns. Turns out deer speak
Anatropically, it figures.

Beasts are good to think with

That animals are better than they
morph to challenge thought

All things change but nothing dies

Fill their ears with wondrous things

I have a very strong instinct

Volta re-
volts

oops
            the reins fell out of my hand

Cursor choose
Rehabit the empty commons
Rabbits rehabit
Forgotten in remembering
Waiting in the cold, beside that gate
Mediating meteor
Polymer
I stand on the mark
Wanna nurse me, you little bitch?

As if they were swine

Caught my Sloppy copyist
Dropping it sopping so

the p's stop popping at the top

They touch very closely upon our subject

Propped up,
Propitiate
Seedcorn

All told

All tell the same story
Then there was an attic, so he goes into the attic
He sees a hole, says shit, what's that
When it grows again
Or which do not grow back?
The nurse is also a mouth needing to be fed
A whirlpool sucking down the water
Chin dripping tears
Changeable and elusive nature
Feign a crook back or limp
Prodding him awake with it
Burnished in the fire
Tossed it up and down in a blanket

And was Nothing but a Prank

Changed into a deer, sounds like a
Person trying to imitate a deer

[*Ahem*, What does a deer]

damaged pronoun

I'll be your food's food

Though I seem tame

I speak for my name in name only

Your name
is a number to
which I cannot count

Stupid fucking browser
Stop bellowing
How wilt my ear hear the hearth's heat

they closed up the mouth of the dark entry

bolt drawn and I do not want the key again

A dog is faithful even to the poor

Do not become attached to the wealthy

Do not bark at poor people

Do not Trip o'er The beat my dark ~~deer~~ no, hart skipped

skipped a
Farthing
Change my changling darling pining
in my oakened hope
Fell into the diamond's grave
w/A phrase from the vulgate

Sithens in a net I seek to ~~wind~~ wind you
A vain travail In letters plain
To draw your last meow, now how
Crack the door to put you out

Of doubt

I'm winded

I may by no means draw me

Tells me to churn it out, I'll feel

butter

Draw straight
               from the deer,   life drawing
To a close, close
This copse, wood a corpse
My cyclops mind hops to cope
Fainting I follow,

Farther Farthing
Draw a card
To Cadge w/
This vain travail hath made me wary
I'm sure sore
Wartorn
corked

On the gurney my gown caught
But it's not my thread
Telltale hart
Deer o deer
Buck up
Download the cumquick.doc
Hartshorn
Thorn pays court to wound
In my lorn
In winter
My content provider
Now is the winter of
My content
Scared of
Scarce half-made
Shaped sportive
Got doored
deered
In ear shot
The template
Is not my heart

This search returns all items

I shall ever do so

tho I must go, whoso would list

No, we are brothers
You belong to me
—Did not boast but showed their scars

With pomp drip gold

Noli me tangerine, Listerine sovereign,
Wolver, or wolver plove
Save to this drive

driven harts from copse closing
Deer Does hélas mean alas

Do I dare to eat

A last salvo drove this driver for to hinding be

My hindsight hunts me down
Sleuthed

To come farthest from behind
And wild for to hold

afore my forelock
loaves antling
cover drivel
Rival
Ravel coeval river

Noli me tangelo

Let me tangle
Tangent
Tangible

for at caesar's palace I wild a card
to put doubt off, perchance
to dream whoso, of hunting fame
I know, though may I by
                          no
Means nec.

We each do game in earnest now

So let us melt and make no noise

I am of them that

I leave off therefore those things that elemented it
To lean and hearken
Wilt thou be so to me, whoso must
Hunt this god-forsaken
Deer I go in circles, thy firmness in my oblique run
My wearied mind can't
compass
Seized with seizing up
sneezing My seasoning, out
of season I am
If a hunter may
undone come
andante
comandante
calm comma
Ever-receding
Fleeth
Seeth
~~Teeth~~ Teeth
Dear deer
Made a salad amid a mid-
caesarian stanza here: here stands a
stand of trees would wood this for rest, rest
now   ever
rest

As for me, I may doth if the other do

I leave off therefore

O range orange range   the wood,   the word?

One-to-one redirects here   here

here

p.s.

When I run

The trees

blur

p.p.s.

When I run

The trees

they

Will stop

barking

Exhausted animals
Why do you run from me
I could hardly catch up

The inkwell's hole
Will sing for your supper

To cover transportation

My new track began to die away

(It snowed so fast)

just put your head on the rack there

let me take your coat

work diary

tore
my face off and

ate it

stupid blunder

hardly recognize myself

      Still in my dressing-gown

the blockade forces us

to improvise

Somebody should do
all my paintings for me

      Keep up the good work

not having seen me again

Good for it

A beast sells a man at a discount,

noting a divot in

the left front hock

It Watches me sullenly from under lowered brows
And lumbers 'cross the rough yard to be petted
cord put in my hand

Do you have it on you?

I praise the winter plum

Caught
in my throt

a version of touch?

I have seen the slain rise, their faces slosh

as a fire dies from a drink of water

I kept my arms raised
                              Above the waves

Not in accordance with duty but from

A certain interest

One says this, and then one hesitates

even

To roughen the surface of words
                With a little punctuation

Page curls, licking its wounds

More fool me

If the fictitious body were a stake and
The real body a beast
Tied to it

Or Gnarled wood emerging from a cloak, as though
It were a hand

           Wood becomes hand

All manner of shortcuts

Here It comes, open,
              and close

To cow me with its blink?, holding
                    a stained paper cup

              "Teach me how to lock up,
            up Like I own the place"

I new pay comma as if not paid before period

Nothing grows bigger than its own seed

We are in a mill

We are in a mill

I fall in love with the millstone

As it is and in its poverty

Innocent as pur-

ée

Took me by the hand and seemed Courteous
            , if
        weary

its donkey grizzled, grist-

less Follows, yet cannot but encircle just one piece of ground

Quotation   Quotation   quotation

Can't complain

            A whole clause has been left out

Can't

Hiding its face in my sleeve, we
leave-take

Emptying the frame

And my arm worn now to threads, we Cling

to every second

That flies away forever;

Snap a shot, its grain

Always turns around too soon

wherefore the earth blow with born corn,

Behind us reach to lift each flattened blade

Time held me green

We had never been there

Wandry

I am in disguise

From my hidey hole
I Broke, breaking through a brake of hawthorn

My gown unhappy with this particular baroque

I felt as though I had found my way

I didn't want to take anything else in

Whereupon we
Hoped   I would be
Changed back
Into the human form we
Had grown accustomed to me in and
Which I had occupied if not well then boldly and
With stout good humor And
So thought we
I deserved my human form

A powerful sense of hop

How may I hop you?

Can I help you?

Let's get started

Push enter so we can begin

I hop about bewildered

I am gray, like ash

Please keep your receipts

To each –ing, its –ness

Dust of its tiny feathers as it brushed

It didn't went over

Rescue workers

Speech, speech, let down your here

Stop this Bullying!

I go here harking

Rude climes?, c'est moi!

You tell your maid to tell me you're not in there

Suture self

The skin is held tightly against your chest

To see if it "goes"

Adulterate night, to shade I turn appeasing

Not that shade!

[Overrided]

But this grift gifted so calcified it cried

Ad hominem I noticed

Mires their bleeding overalls

The gag tied too tightly

Wit' a sickass click

Take any remedy who I command my sicks

Now, that's not friendlike fire

Get me my armor or

You're yore, you're storied

Locked up in that moment

The page you requested has moved
Mr. father

So I've created this neutral space between realms

Funny deficit
Honey you're running a
rough total

You with the fliers at the intersection of

You've given me shit Shrift

You can season this rookie
While I smile for the Camaro

This we buy, this we take without paying

I now pronounce this swaddling closed

Tunneling

Get out   There's no more room

Then how could I have come in?

Don't argue

Thus it was when I was in my mother's worm

Show your stubs!

They don't wave back

My cereal soggeth

The animals came out at dusk, looking for food

I had found forage to Hit me up for:

'Scuse me surrounding myself with foodstuffs,
these moveables, lunchables

Come hither, my shiver amn't the chivalry of a silvery herring

Smoothing the cloth over my lap, over lapping

Then with ladle poured soup 'til my hands overflew

My mandible and itchy trigger pincers

Cl'cl'clinging the tongue's sticky work

I had a good time, with no regrets

Ok, now 'scuse you

This is family time
Like puppies, the children fall down on top of each other with pleasure
Their faces stick to the floor They have to rip their heads off

Mother helps

Shifting its weight

Man is a speaking animal but
The owl,
            the owl

Turns its head all the way
around

All volcanoes in favor, say

It was not originally intended for that

Includes airfare and first-class arachnids

Mezzanines

Neither flesh nor fowl

They are let loose, run loose

Jaywalked so much the fence wore away

My labors crush me smooth as a shell

hygiene?, hmph

let me pull myself together

wait! Maybe this does not concern me

more sniggering

the menials surround me critically

congers gnashing and champing emptily

"And when and how pleaseth

janitor scrapes their gum from the floor

I too grip the world's edge, set my fingers to tear

fucking sinkholes bunching it

fall unpitied in the snare

made

By hurting my enemy I hurt my

Of punches rolled w/ and
Fell in the drink for

To belabor this:

Double parked
Clubbed my kennel
Freezerburn

Never give a sucker an even break

He'll break even

He'll

the only exception would be if you can

Topiary

Like a candle nervously aware of its melting

I hawked up death from my throat

Who really know how to dies

Broke winged, flutt'ring half-circles in
The dirt
Spraying furrows in earth's brow
Confused

Or listening to music that turns its listeners to stone

Or a cat turning round to mark a hollow for sleep

And of whom there's no, no consorting with

You're a marked man, no I'm

A bit wide of the kram, ma'am

I can't stand it, I can't
Stand

I command

the ivy to cover it over

(sob)
'Til daybreak announce mourning to me

I will not mourn

P.S. I came back as a shrubbery

I led a life there suitable to my temper

Copying music at so much per page

Instructional aid

Permit me to say a word about

Your being shall rehearse a necessary assumption
This 'twill sling proudly over its shoulder

w/Endearing Awkwardness

and This roll call in the rocky crags Carves you out from the blank
planetary surround It will personify you anonymously, Then

This is not worth explaining

They are right

They are right who say "Love is hounded to the ends of the earth"

If you prick us, prick, do we not bled?

Bed completely bedraggled
shuffling in a back room,
And withdrew into its secret

Yet holding nothing back

I crooked my finger and beckoned me

I don't enjoy cornering like this—

I'll cottage you but don't imagine I enjoy

Depths out of which one does not rise again

Do you like more the instant of waking or that of falling asleep?

And this would be a kind of proof?

A holiness that resillence lowly stole me to, slowly

blinking in the dark of its belly

And wait with bited breast

Sorry to keep you waiting

Humming to console me

we were our own solarity
At this intimate scale

It scratched my heart and made it itch but I

I resolved not to tell anyone of it

Instead, to whisper in the hollow of a tree

This tattling restored my naïvety

At the crest of the rising

Someone jogged by,

I thought, Get Heart Smart

Forestalling need at the breakdown of its adequacy

A room rented in an inn

Is hungry; eats a lot

At the end of the meal, fog before my eyes, reptiles on the floor

Rise, Peter; kill and eat

Eats more

Intestines very long, too long

Quail not Trussed

The arrowy radiations of a toothache

Ah, If one only accustoms oneself to

Never mind that!

This disobedience slept (snoring)

Dreaming, sees

a man seated in full light in a corner of the room,

the reptiles have disappeared

The man says, *Don't eat so much.*

My warm and well-merited indignation

Gasping at saws

Scene: a hillock of earth

The bee may be laden and skip the flower.

The drawing mocked its own cross-hatching.

Squints.

You, too? I asked.

weak messianic power

The poem will be held today

Language permitting

Or what it can actually tell us

I'm it   yet
I'm only a repetition
Performing it, not quoting it
allegory stock, or stalk,
                          was   it
                          stick
          rabid ibid pre-
          cipits incipit
          Pet me, I lick

          Where my voice was used for this

Read this word next
unto and against   aslant is like
How they talk when aslant or Sitting
          The hand is an idea. Both legs: ideas.

Whereof one speaks   but

What then is time

If no one asks me, I know
If I want to explain it, I do not know
And yet I know

What then is time

No one asks me

if I want to explain it

I don't know,
you know?

We none of us

this black debt

Father kills himself to spare his son the task

Pray you undo this button
Come and be dead

Putting my weight into the thicker downstroke

I'm your taker

that at
one or two
removes The
removes
are more important

There is nothing

There is nothing
common to all games

as When something is repeated another instance
of that something comes into   existence

as When a child throws his ball at the wall and catches it again
On this page and copies of this page
Of which there are yet no copies

I have no character

Or whatever they regard as the same
Being decided to be, Or recognized as

the character discusses a theory of fictional utterances
these are differences of the same sign
a mere instance
to which it belongs

as When it is said, someone O
pened Pandora's box, it
does not
usually
mean he or she opened Pandora's box

as When a king granted his own arm unlimited power

It has no meaning without that counterpart
Similar arrangements were made

Tenfold

Do you see what I mean?

How clad and shod, The final row overlaps
            truth's chamber will not close—
Now all we've learnt, in vain?

With reference to the wrong things, the obvious things,
I purchase my authority with

with a breach so large that

            . The narrative line has turned inwards
blood for blood but not done yet
            In arrears
to itself,   Ransoming its own succession,
it Fills out the separate forms,
channels dug Fate verbatim
Thrusts like a shadow, freighted
With each other's Slowing down˙

Eyes adjust

That which suffers in the soul,
fullness or emptiness?

These words thrown away?

Lost when spoken or
controlled by more words?

Back miscopies forth

as When a child, his ball

any Pretended act is logically posterior

folds in against a goblet's hollow
or The heavy look of marble folds

You darn your ankles with ink
As they peek   Through a threadbare sock

My own words cited against me?,
Yet forefend return

This, my coefficient,
Between non-coincident ends

　　　　　There were many empty rooms

　　　　　Some are barely scraps

I am tired of examples but

I'll disappear when I stop

We none of us

　　　　　　　　　　　This black debt

it does not say who

Who is Pandora
She opened a box
Or pretended to, by
engaging in pretense
naked in its Plumes
its own form of act

still had I hopes of forgiveness
to cite my own words against me

putting my weight in the thicker downstroke

on this page and copies of this page

      Where my voice was used for this

Pet me   *Pray*
you undo this button   Read
"this word" next. Whereof one speaks,
needs are defective,
that obtain in them, if thinly

To pay for the upkeep
Not as morning, but as noon;
word Cut from word

A breach so large   stock-
holms
reciprocal being,
a series of mishaps
common to all games.
How clad, shod, The final row overlaps
Made to fear home and stray

Plastic and detachable, subwoofed in
exhausted shapes

Take off their jackets and mop their foreheads

I don't know,

what do you want here, Idler,
who let you in?
my fingers trembling on the lid

the smaller act contains the larger act
I'm coated with sweet kernels

"I'm coated with sweet kernels"
Will be in a peculiar way hollow or void
If introduced
                    in a poem

Save   save this one thing Save
my place   This note refers to any "place" in the text

If you are here
If you are here and would,
as When

as When we

as When we
still

~~don't~~

know how

much

~~less~~

nothing

can

be

The Waste Line [a'cursed share]

Similarly eggs can be made to talk

I made an egg talk and it confessed utterly

At a social gathering such as this

       shades slightly into acting—

Egg butts in, auspicy
       You don't yoke an egg to a

The thing what lies in the method of presenting it
Since anything can stand in for anything else
To inhabit as a motion
And which I can only trust to you
Opens at my invisible self & exhibits me in a world of true infinity

Shreds dangling,
        from the edges of forms

The dog is moved by beauty. Subservience
I'm not going to make it easy for you
As I though I were nature slumbering
Onto which words could fasten and begin
Like snaps upon a shirtface

Hold my stupid hand

Hold open the hole

I have to do an errand

Will you carry me

Darkly, but then face to face

of us gloved and scarved, flapping dumbly

Cancel all adverbs

So event can reabsorb

Smile

you're

a candied camera

                        I yam?

[untitled]

~~penguins don' swi~~   penguins
do swi, the,y don't fli-
ckr off cliffs any
quickr than Icar-
us did. the Briny Deep
do penguins Swim

Earth
lies fl.at
but so
does
heaven
lie, I
~~spi~~. spy.
See, no
more kiss
the poles
as they
cros.s.
crying
they cry,
north star
by South,
giving a briny
          light.
but,   With
their eyes
x'ed out.

extension Cord

& say to the moment, this very moment, stay you are so fair, what will be one's gain, dying? No: stay, this moment. No one ever says that enough. Always hurry.

Virginia Woolf, diary (Dec. 31, 1932)

All that one can give is what is going to happen, which may have little to do with a present that you can grasp.

Avital Ronell, *Finitude's Score*

And why should they bother to help with anything the world takes seriously? After all, it's nothing but madness. They prefer to take walks. And if they encounter a dog or some living creature on their walks, they whisper: "I have nothing to give you, dear animal; I would gladly give you something, if only I had it." Nevertheless, in the end, they lie down in a meadow to weep bitterly over their "stupid greenhorn's existence."

Giorgio Agamben, "The Assistants"

Because, in the event, if you do not want to, you won't.

George Oppen, "Route"

(What will I do?)

————————

S

Mary Kelly, *POST PARTUM DOCUMENT*

In this poem

Let us part

        And if I let you go, should it

                              not have something of its own?

You will continue to receive the same as before

We won't see each other again

To which I held myself

cupboard's bare, not e-
ven a grain of rice   well,

one,

        only one grain of rice

The control text

Choked by undergrowth Int-
erior to words/Words
torn
     from sense, then

fetch the means
from there,

Deleted vicinities, bitch who

eats her young

Do your share

Go through with it   Do
it

I have a single fin and swim
in circles

I'm working on it, im-
itating work

I went in and did it

like a job   In a single take

Leaves it open;

What it will come to, or Wondering

what has become of it

It falls to you

To those who come looking for it,
At the hands of:

When inner speech is silenced, Left
out of the explanation

(ivy clings to the Oak,

Just get it over with!)

If it is written Sunset, or
Sunset's Jagged

Make do.

This is not to be looked at closely,
not asked to Serve concepts

Do not give it sustained attention

Snap it

off, like the end of a bean

                    de-fragged and the weight of robes,
A blur in language clings

To the bare Outside of this world

Ahead of a fullness, ask-
ing it
           of you,

Shower of meteors
on the dirty wall

A Little Chestnut

grape sits sullen, looking sour

behind every cave, there is another Deeper cave

Clothes that leave us bare

I lost my cellphone &

I lost my cellphone &

My tongue cries out like a living thing
Or A little gilt-edged book

Wresting the lower genre
It hatched and set free

My sparrow is go for to keep his cut
Unneth, I cast mine

swallowing my tail

Or the rental pair

Come what may

A goose spoke with a human voice

The voice laid golden ears

I hid in a pile of leaves and slept

Taken merely
for Firmament

From the outset

to cry)(before the prick

my Now)(inside of yours

I run)(after (something
I am not sure)(about it

Yes, come,)(we must pick up speed

The bruce

Rag picker Drawing
in the air with a finger

Of this oft-consulted page

       Where dost you take your Lodgings

       Let me draw up the bill

Closing the door behind   (keeping tabs)

Meaning devours,

Grows dissipated
          and bloat

An ill-gotten gain

Backwardsness can be looked back

Worked out on a piece of paper At

treeline, atremble   Trying

to get close to the fire

clenched fist or open palm?

Reeling back the string without its kite

or, Door, with a slit for the mail
Minus truth

The rest missing, too,

Veteran

[untitled]

sea has no score

behind the roar

Father on the beach,

calling to the referents,

stay on the shore

You must

You must no longer wander

Your grave

is here "

"

[YOUR DATA HAS BEEN SENT

[TRACKBACKS CLOSED

Post-face: On "l.b." & catenaries [slack-s]

l.b. = Wordsworth and Coleridge, *Lyrical Ballads* (1798)

In his Preface to *Lyrical Ballads* (1800), Wordsworth describes his book as an aesthetic, moral project—"an experiment...to ascertain how far, by fitting to metrical arrangement a selection of the real language of men in a state of vivid sensation," poetry may impart its peculiar pleasure to the reader.

l.b.; or, catenaries is thick in conversation with that project. It attempts to renovate it for the 21st century, though with the caveat that it is all too aware of "aesthetic competence and ineffectuality in the face of the world's larger realities" (James E. Young, *At Memory's Edge*), however these realities may come into view by means of the underdetermined, interrupted, and partial micro-vignettes presented here.

Like Wordsworth, then, I am interested in conveying and perhaps manipulating affect through language. Like him, I'm in search of tones (musical and attitudinal) and postures that are both the quotidiana and marginalia of contemporary existence. I'm drawn to the chafing, the awkward, the threadbare, the shaming and belittling, the angry, and the lowly comic—as to prickly self-consciousness and seemingly less conscious self-aggrandizement.

For all my fascination, and sickness with, postmodern forms of social negativity, these poems desire and reflect the near-impossibility of social rupture. They explore the many ways *we fail to fall out of relation* even as minimized and maximized connection becomes messy, violent, and incoherent. So, too, these poems enact the impossibility of stability or uniformity in any cathexis, prying open (sometimes unexpected) ambivalences. They shadow the continual jostling, giddiness, dysfunction, and hypersensitivity precipitated by multiplying our self-emanations as we add virtual layer upon virtual layer.

Wordsworth's (not Coleridge's) poems were further experimental in avoiding what he saw as the overly artificial rhetorical figure of apostrophe. As an invocation and performative entification of an addressed "presence," apostrophe helps to create a lyrical time and space, the "here" and "now" of the poem. (On this point, see Jonathan Culler's essay "Apostrophe.") In *Lyrical Ballads*, Wordsworth preferred recollection of a stable past, however concerned he also was with the relation of such telling to his present audience.

With a symptomatic perversity, my poems stage a return of what Wordsworth was wont to repress, fixating on the reality-effects of the chronic, bewildering deictic triggers in this age of automated text and speech act. They hold up for scrutiny how desublimated, radicalized figures—tropes that underscore their own artifice or empty, functional provisionality—reveal the tenacity of sentiment, subjectivity, and voice, rather than producing detachment. I am interested, too, in our loss of control over the linguistic manufacture of presence, and in the absurd but consequential referentiality among the levels of an indeterminate manifold of frames.

Though the poems here are not written in meter, they attend, perhaps more than to the concerns raised above, to sound and especially to rhythm: to the creation of social topology through timing and pacing. These are retardant poems. They reflect and produce non-standardizable speeds.

catenary: *n. Math.* The curve formed by a chain or rope of uniform density hanging freely from two fixed points not in the same vertical line. (*OED*)

I use the catenary as a metaphor for the lyric relations developed here. It points up my sense of the poems' predicament of immediacy and extreme mediatedness. A catenary's arc is a figure of excess: it joins two points, but with slack between them (a swerve). Yet this inscription embodies a "natural" self-sufficiency: nothing intervenes to tauten the half-loop gravity forms.

"Catenary" comes from "catena," Latin for "chain," surely a charged term in the context of utterance. As Mladen Dolar writes in *A Voice and Nothing More*: "If signifiers form a chain, the voice may well be what fastens them." Again, excess: the voice as material support, the voice as guarantor and vector of intention. Dolar is, perhaps, building on Lacan's dictum in "The Agency of the Letter in the Unconscious" that, "It is in the chain of the signifier that the meaning 'insists.'"

Yet in the same essay Lacan also defies this sense of wholeness in the not-one, that outside-language on which meaning depends; he declares a polyphonic, dispersive, rather than linear, vocality or meaningfulness for the chain. "One has only to listen to poetry," he states, "…for a polyphony to be heard, for it to become clear that all discourse is aligned along the several staves of a score…There is in effect no signifying chain that does not have…a whole articulation of relevant contexts suspended 'vertically.'"

Natural/figural, singular/plural, abstract/concrete, sufficiency/slack—all differences put under erasure by Jasper Johns' *Catenary* series. At once painting and sculptural object, Johns' masterful *Near the Lagoon*, for instance, features a literal cord hanging freely between points on the canvas; this same cord is remarked in a negative impression in the work's thick encaustic, in drawn curves representing it, and in the literal shadow it throws on the surface of the canvas.

I see the catenary, too, as the text mediating the temporal gap between the time of writing and the time of reading. As the clew stringing a déjà lu text to its next appropriation. The thread from irony to pathos.

End Notes

Poems in this book have been written over the last seven years. Lines and phrases from many, many sources have here been lifted—changed, unchanged, reanimated or made "less dead" (to use the words of painter Marlene Dumas), zombified, killed and rekilled. I do not want to, nor can I, escape these heavy debts, yet it would be clumsy, projective recollection to attempt to list them all.

I am a scavenger: George Oppen once asserted his citations "are not allusions; they are thefts"; Franz Kafka stated, "I am made of literature."

Dust to dust. Letter to letter. Spark to spark.

*   *   *

Itt is said, hee had noe ill intencion, noe ill harte, but hee maye bee ill interpreted. That must not bee allowed him in excuse, for hee should not have written any thinge that would bear [that] construccion, for hee doth not accompanye his booke, to make his intencion knowne to all that reades it.

Star Chamber, proceedings against William Prynne, 1634